HALSTEAL
COLNE VALLEY AT WAR
(1939 - 1945)

by
DAVE OSBORNE

On 23rd April, 1944 Vivien Leigh, Laurence Olivier and other stage personalities went to Ridgewell to see Mary Churchill (daughter of Winston Churchill) christen 'Stage Door Canteen' A bottle of coke on the nose guns did the job.

© Copyright Dave Osborne, 1983   **£4.50**
© Second (revised) edition copyright Dave Osborne 1992.

I.S.B.N. 0 9513106 7 4

Published by the Halstead and District Local History Society.
Printed by Ron Bussey Printers, Hobtoes Farm, Stambourne Road, Finchingfield, Essex.

Further copies available from the author, Dave Osborne 47 Dooley Road, Halstead, Essex or from Adrian Corder-Birch, "The Maltings", North End Road, Little Yeldham, Halstead, Essex CO9 4LE. Price £4.50 plus 60p postage and packing.

PREFACE TO SECOND (REVISED) EDITION

by Adrian Corder-Birch, F.Inst.L.Ex., M.I.C.M.,
Chairman of Halstead and District Local History Society

During the last fifteen years the Halstead and District Local History Society have published no less than fifteen books on various aspects of Local History. Some of the earlier books are now out of print and without doubt Dave Osborne's book 'Halstead and Colne Valley at War, (1939-1945)' has been one of the most successful. Although two thousand copies of the first edition were printed sales were so good that all copies were sold within four years. Since then the demand for this popular book has been so great that the author, Dave Osborne, and the Halstead and District Local History Society, as publishers, have jointly decided to have this second (revised) edition printed.

Dave Osborne has enjoyed a vast amount of correspondence with American servicemen since this book was first published in 1983. He is a member of the Friends of the 381st Bomb Group who were based at Ridgewell Airfield and is one of the principal local organisers for visits to this area by former American airmen.

His great enthusiasm for researching the history of the Second World War in the Halstead area has made him many friends not only in this country but around the world. His continuing research must surely result in a new volume one day.

The Foreword for the first edition, which is reprinted here, was written by Sir Ronald Long who sadly passed away in 1987. Sir Ronald, who was President and later Patron of the Halstead and District Local History Society was a well known Solicitor. He was Clerk to the Halstead Urban District Council for forty years including the war years, when he was also Food Executive Officer and Chief Reception Officer for evacuees in Halstead. Sir Ronald was also Commanding Officer of No. 1163 Squadron, Colne Valley Air Training Corps. His service to the town of Halstead was unique. The inspiration and assistance he gave Dave Osborne and other local authors was unparalleled.

The successful publishing programme of the Halstead and District Local History Society for which a firm foundation has been given by Sir Ronald Long, Dave Osborne and others will undoubtedly continue during the ensuing years.

Adrian Corder-Birch

The Maltings, Little Yeldham, Halstead, Essex.   January, 1992

AUTHOR'S ACKNOWLEDGMENTS

I would like to express my grateful thanks to the following who have helped me with information and photographs to compile this book:

Diane Adams
Mary Argent
Percy A. L. Bamberger
Cyril Ball
Sid Basford
Rev. Kenneth F. Belben, T.D., C.F.
Ted Beard
Mrs. Bennett
Beatrice M. Birch
Mollie Bishop
Bert Bragg
Rev. Brian Carew, A.I.B.
Adrian Corder-Birch, F.Inst.L.Ex.,
Jack Cornell
Major Eric Crabbe
Jean Crabbe
Albert Cross
John Cribb
Rev. Peter C. Ford
Roy Giller
George Green
Mike Hall
Eddie Heavingham

Elsie Hillier
Canon A. Stuart J. Holden, A.L.C.D.,
Mrs. Ingram
Arthur Kelson
Pat King
Beryl Knight
F. Norah Lambert
Sir Ronald Long
Paul Maytham
Brenda Noble
Ronald Parr
Rev. C. D. G. Patterson, Dip. Th., A.C.I.I.
Bill Petty
Major Michael Portway
Geoff Root
Dick Ruggles
Elizabeth Smith
Brenda Stebbing
Alethea M. Waller
Maurice Wickens
Eric White
The Archivist and staff of the
Essex Record Office

I would particularly like to thank Percy Bamberger, Adrian Corder-Birch and Geoffrey Root who have read the script and given much useful help and advice and to Sir Ronald Long who has written the Foreword.

My grateful thanks are also due to Colne Valley Printers Limited for printing and John Abbott, Dave Barker and Ken Stanhope for reproducing the photographs for this book.

Last but not least to my wife Jo-Anne who has suffered with my absence and many telephone calls goes my grateful appreciation.

Dave Osborne
Halstead, Essex, 1983

FOREWORD

by Sir Ronald Long

Dave Osborne has remembered them with pride and sympathy.

After nearly four decades he has, with great patience, devotion and meticulous research, presented us with this stirring and absorbing history of Halstead and the Colne Valley at War. He draws pictures of the unfailing loyalty, patriotism and sacrifice which inspired the whole community through the dark times of Hitler's War. No call to any form of duty was unanswered. High morale and comradeship abounded and with steadfast determination led to the well deserved victory in 1945. The reader will find references to the then novel conditions brought about by war in the air and will as he reads, see pictures of evacuees and troops arriving, of soldiers and airmen on duty and hear the noise in our Essex skies from enemy attack and combat. He will learn of the service which was so gladly given and of those who made the supreme sacrifice. Fortunately many were "welcomed home."

Those who were here between 1939 and 1945 will be rewarded by renewing graphic memories of the past and everyone will be proud to read of our district's grand record during this trying epoch. Dave Osborne richly deserves the warmest thanks and support which I am sure he will receive.

I commend his history to you.

Halstead
Essex

6th September 1983

It is just as well that Adolf Hitler did not have a grudge against Halstead or this story might not have been written.

With the rumbling over Europe, Halstead and the Colne Valley did not show too much concern. There was no heavy industry or docks to be bombed, for this quiet corner of North Essex was given over to agriculture in all its forms.

However it was in September 1938 that the political situation over the German-Czechoslovakia dispute showed signs of worsening, and air raid precautions were very much in the forefront of the public's mind.

A special meeting was called at the Queens Hall seeking volunteers and the local branch of the ARP (Air Raid Precautions) was formed under the leadership of Mr. Ted Parker, but the chief warden was Col. Hills of Chipping Hill, Halstead, the HQ being the former Police Barracks that stood at the foot of Mount Hill opposite the Chapel Hill junction.

The town was divided into 22 sections, but here superstition must have ruled, for there was no No. 13!

The sections and wardens were:
1-T. G. N. Franklin; both sides of Sudbury Road, from Colne Road to town boundary, Colne Road north sides to entrance to Coggeshall Pieces (Ramsey School staff entrance).

2-Harry Sturmer; Head Street from Colchester Road corner to Colne Road corner east side; Chipping Hill; Manfield Highbury Terrace, Crown Yard (now demolished); Morley Road; Pretoria Road; East Mill; Colne Road south side from Head Street to the Bellrope Field (rough land next to the cemetery) and Colchester Road, north side from Head Street corner to Bellrope Field.

3-Cyril Evans; Colne Road both sides from Bellrope Field to Fenn corner; Fenn Road to Colchester Road corner and north side of Colchester Road.

4-George Preece; Colchester Road south side from Roman Catholic church to Fenn Road corner; Middlefield and both sides Colchester Road from Fenn Road corner to the railway.

5-Francis Adams; Colchester Road south side from Mallows Field to Roman Catholic church; Mallows Field east side from Colchester Road to Weavers Row; Harvey Street and Weavers Row.

6-Sidney Pole; Parsonage Street, south west from White Horse to railway crossing and Factory Lane East.

7-Will Collier; Colchester Road south side from Head Street, west side of Mallows Field, High Street east side from White Horse in Parsonage Street.

8-Leo Lindekam; High Street south east side from White Hart to River Bridge; Gatehouse Yard; Factory Lane East and Vicarage Meadow.

9-Henry Pountney; High Street north west from Chapel Street to River Bridge; both sides Chapel Street from Paper Mill (long black wooden building used as industrial store) up to Balham House (top of Upper Chapel Street).

10-C. Westrop; High Street north west from Chapel Street to Hedingham Road; Chapel Street from High Street to Bay House (replaced by flats); Hedingham Road from Market Hill to The Moyes (allotments opposite hospital); Boars Head Yard, Belle Vue; and Oakleigh and Balham Houses.

11-Reg Tanswell; Hedingham Road

1

both sides from Cottage Hospital to The Howe; Hepworth Hall; Fitzjohns Farm and Broakes House (in Broakes Wood).

12-Jack Salmon; Hedingham Road, east side from Bois Field Terrace to Cottage Hospital; Mill Chase; Head Street north west side from School Lane to Colne Road corner.

14-V. G. Cross; Head Street north west side from Market Hill to School Lane; north east side of Hedingham Road from Head Street to and including Bois Field Terrace; Fleece Yard; Chase Yard; Rose Yard and School Lane, south west side.

15-Miss Patch; Tidings Hill, south west side from railway to UDC boundary (towards Bourne Brook) including Stones Farm and Balls Chase.

16-Bill Knowles; Kings Road, both sides from Tidings Hill to Mitchell Avenue; Tidings Hill, north west side from railway to UDC boundary; Great Yard (now demolished); Cherry Yard; School Chase and Boyces (next to Rayner Way) and Mitchell Avenue, south east side.

17-Alec Watkinson; Kings Road from Mitchells Avenue to Trinity Street, New Street, south west side; Neale Road, south west side; Mitchell Avenue, north west side; Trinity Road north east side from Mount Hill to Mount Pleasant, then both sides from Trinity Road down to New Street.

19-Sidney Tomlinson; Trinity Road, south west side from Mount Hill to Mount Pleasant, including the bungalow off Trinity Road (home of Mr. Morton Newton, but now demolished); Mount Pleasant both sides from Trinity Road to top; Summers Row (now demolished); Upper Trinity Road, and Mount Hill south east side from Trinity Road to UDC

boundary (near to Blamsters Farm entry).

20-Jack Simmons; Mount Hill, north west side from Chapel Hill to UDC boundary, including Blamsters Farm; Chapel Hill, south west side from Mount Hill to Crowbridge Farm.

21-Arthur Buck; Beridge Road, north west side from railway to Crowbridge Farm; Sloe Hill both sides to UDC boundary; Sloe House, lodge and farm and both sides Stanley Road.

22-Stanley Symonds; Rosemary Lane; Bridge Street both sides from railway crossing to town Bridge, and the Causeway.

The meeting also heard that Mr. R. A. Butler, MP, had offered Stansted Hall as a hospital, and could provide a six bed ward within 24 hours, and another in 48 hours.

Some 20,000 gas masks had been recently delivered from London and about 100 Courtaulds girls began the task of assembling them, with the distribution of some of them taking place that same evening.

In January 1939 a communique was issued by the Minister of Health, Walter Elliott, asking local authorities to put in hand immediately a survey of all accommodation suitable for the reception of children and other persons who might be removed from dangerous areas in case of war.

Halstead Urban District Council duly obliged and the clerk, Ronald Long announced rates of 10/6d (52½p) per week for one child, and 8/6d each child thereafter; adults 5/- and 3/- for each of the children with them. The town was split into three sections for this purpose, under: Sidney Pole, Jack Simmons and Bob Minter.

In March the ARP called for emergency cover for transport and 22 operators volunteered 51 vehicles, under the charge of Mr. H. P. Newman (of Newman & Clark, now Dalgety Spillers, in Kings Road).

The following month saw a national appeal for young men to join the Territorial Army. A meeting was called and a parade was assembled at Wash Farm in Hedingham Road which was headed by the police and TA band, and marched to the Public Gardens where Mr. R.A. Butler called for volunteers.

Four interview panels were set up: Charlie Ready in New Street; Miss Patch, of the WVS at Nether Priors; Francis Adams, at the Brewery, Trinity Street (now council offices) and Harry Hughes, in Chapel Street. There was quite a good response in the next few weeks with 49 joining in Halstead and 21 at Earls Colne. By June another 67 signed on in Halstead

In July the ARP held two training exercises, one at Frost's Mill, where a high explosive bomb had fallen, and at Fenn Road where three gas bombs fell. After the 'All Clear' the men assembled at St. Andrews School (then in Colchester Road), where Inspector Mallows of the HQ at Chelmsford commented on the exercise and answered questions.

At the beginning of August, commanding officer of the ARP, Capt Evans Hemming, appointed the previous year, announced a blackout exercise was to be held in the town between midnight and 4am on the 10th. Householders were urged to make certain all curtains were secured and the public were requested to keep vehicles off the road as all the street lights would be extinguished, not that there were many vehicles in Halstead back in 1939 Capt Hemming also announced that some 30,000 gas masks were stored.

In their infinite wisdom, the Home Office allocated another tender for the local fire brigade, and Halstead Urban District Council requested that two emergency telephone lines be installed, adding that the surveyor should arrange the necessary drills. A few days later an advertisement appeared in the Halstead Gazette calling for volunteers for the fire brigade.

Further requests were made calling for the public to find accommodation to billet troops which were gradually being stationed around the country.

Life was going on as normal despite the politicians and their arguments, with the Four Colnes Show set for 19 August complete with Greenways Electric Fair, and a Fete and Sports Day at Belchamp Walter.

Next in the preparations for war came the order from the Registrar General that identity cards were to be issued, ready for a national register, but only in the event of a war.

The men of Halstead had already been 'Doing their bit' including the Territorial Army who paraded at the Drill Hall in Pretoria Road (now Kingdom Hall of Jehovahs Witnesses).

The Halstead detachment was part of the 2/5th Battalion of the Essex Regiment and was formed in the early Nineteen Thirties. It consisted mainly of Halstead and Earls Colne men with a few from the Hedinghams, 17 being fully trained who were joined by 70 recruits. They were taught by Sgts Ron Wicker and Bill Howe who were the mainstays of Pretoria Road Drill Hall for some years. PSI Bob Coe was the drill instructor.

3

Various forms of weapon training and exercises were held under the eagle eye of experienced NCOs and by March 1939 the numbers had risen to make Halstead a full company.

In May the 5th Battalion was divided into two; Colonel Cedric Portway taking command of the newly formed 2/5th. Captain Gerald Clover was 'B' Company Commander, and platoon commanders were 2nd Lt Paul Maytham, 2nd Lt Jim Porter and Sgt Alf Binks MM; platoon Sgts being Dick Stedman, Bert Bragg and Eddie Cook.

The company went through months of weapon training as the rumblings over Europe grew louder. The Army ranges at Colchester echoed to the sounds of rifle and bren gun fire, and with a variety of marksmen behind the triggers, the butt markers had their problems! However, the company eventually progressed to reach the final of the Battalion Rifle Championships but failed to land the trophy.

Highlight of the T.A. year was the annual camp which was usually spent at an army camp, and the last before hostilities began was held at Wannock, near Eastbourne, during the first two weeks of August.

At Braintree 'C' Company was formed under Captain A. J. Hills, in April 1939 and included many local men, the inauguration being celebrated by a recruiting march which began at Castle Hedingham, through Sible Hedingham, to Halstead where they heard stirring words of encouragement from Mr. R. A. Butler, then Under Secretary of State, before ending their march at Earls Colne. 'A' Company was from the Colchester area.

Through August the political pressure was building up and hourly announcements came over the radio for men to report for duty according to age groups and names.

'B' Company of the 2/5th were actually on a route march in the Black Notley vicinity when war broke out. They had reported for duty a couple of days previously when the plumbers, carpenters, bricklayers and others dropped their tools and made for the Drill Hall complete with uniforms and equipment. They were met by senior NCOs, themselves awaiting orders, and the men slept in the Drill Hall that night.

Within weeks the men of 'B' Company found themselves at Warners Holiday Camp at Dovercourt, where they began preparing for war in earnest. But that is another story . . . (for list of personnel see Appendix V).

At 11am on 3rd September the Prime Minister, Neville Chamberlain announced "I have received no reply from Germany, and a state of war now exists between us."

It made little difference to the people of Halstead and district who went about their daily business as usual, apart from the Colne Valley Cinema now the Chinese Take Away in Trinity Street, which had been temporarily closed under an Emergency Order.

The first attempt to attack Great Britain came on the following Wednesday when German aircraft were driven off apparently intending to attack East Anglia.

In the meantime air raid sirens had been installed throughout the United Kingdom, and in Halstead on the site of the old fire station in Head Street (now the small industrial complex next to the former Napiers Arms). Halsteadians will never forget that mournful wail, the warbling or intermittant warning of an ensuing raid, or the continuous note of the all clear.

By this time people had erected air raid shelters at their homes. Remember the Anderson or the Morrison? Who ever would fail to forget the times mum took the kids downstairs in the middle of the night, to hide under the table?

I well remember when I lived on Mount Pleasant, how my father, Jack Osborne, assisted by several neighbours including Con Carter and Jim Cook, dug a shelter in the back garden large enough for about a dozen. This exercise was repeated tens of thousands of times all over the country.

Bureaucracy enjoyed a field day back in those dark times with the Queens Hall taken over as a centre for the registration of mothers and young children evacuated to the town, while similar arrangements were made at Earls Colne village hall, Castle and Sible Hedingham Womens Institute Hall, Steeple Bumpstead Moot Hall and Foxearth church hall.

With the influx of extra people, many from London, the HUDC issued water conservancy plans, which included the cutting off of the supply at 9.30 each evening. The surveyor reporting that the Waterworks in Parsonage Street had been suitably protected by sandbags, and the workers were each issued with a steel helmet.

Car insurances were extended for people carrying out Civil Defence duties and cyclists were warned to shield their lights in a similar manner to motorists.

As a guide to the residents who took in soldiers for lodging, the Army Act specified that: bed for the night with no cooking - 6d; with meals, breakfast - 8d; dinner - 11d; tea - 3d and supper - 5d. Various food prices were announced and had to be strictly adhered to.

Mrs. R. A. Butler headed the Womens Voluntary Service providing a nursery for children at the rear of Lloyds Bank, while the manager of the Westminster Bank, Mr. R. T. Brown offered the use of the bank garden as a playground for children.

The teachers of the district were catered for by the offer by Canon Curling of St. Andrews Hall, Halstead, for use as a clubroom and perhaps a game of cards or darts.

Local allotment holders were asked to play their part in the struggle by growing their own vegetables. Remember the slogan 'Dig for Victory? It was estimated by the boffins that the produce of a normal size allotment (whatever a normal size allotment was in those days) would keep a man, his wife and three children in potatoes and vegetables for 212 days out of the 365.

Some 500 evacuees arrived in Halstead from Waltham Cross, to be met by Ronald Long, chief reception officer, who was also Food Executive Officer. Five busloads arrived about noon and were then directed to the Council Senior School (now Richard De Clare) to be sub-divided into one of the 21 sections for lodging into which Halstead had been split. The arrangements were carried out by the Rating Officer, Reg Rayner.

In the evening more arrived from Enfield and Wood Green and throughout the next few days some

4,000 people swelled the population of the Colne Valley. They were broken down thus: Halstead Urban 1,836; Sible Hedingham 670; Castle Hedingham 214; Gestingthorpe 60; Earls Colne 406; Gosfield 164; Steeple Bumpstead 162; Great Maplestead 17; Little Maplestead 32; Foxearth 60; while Stisted, Cornish Hall End, Finchingfield, Blackmore End and Pattiswick as well as Halstead Rural all played their part.

In October came the news that Bernard Roebuck of Wallaces Farm, Little Maplestead, serving in the Royal Navy at Rosyth, was killed when German aircraft bombed the shipyard, damaging several ships. He was 19. A War Department telegram arriving with a knock at the door was to bring dread to many a heart throughout the land.

The rolling acres of agricultural north Essex did not appeal to all the evacuees and by December nearly 200 decided to risk the Blitz by returning home to the big cities, being unable to settle down.

On 9th December a Royal Proclamation decreed that men between 20-23 shall be called up, and should register at the Queens Hall, complete with identity card.

Despite the war and the impending gloom Halstead continued to make Christmas arrangements, several local dignitaries providing facilities for the evacuees. Fund raising activities for the War Effort saw a Grand Whist Drive and Dance at the Co-op Hall, when 160 people attended to raise funds for the Welfare Mothers party.

Harry Hughes, the local insurance agent announced in the Halstead Gazette that £82/2/7d was raised from the collection of silver foil, for Halstead Hospital, and the Pebmarsh British Legion's womens section had agreed to knit 300 balaclavas.

A Wakes Colne family received new that their son, Sgt F.G. Goodwin, serving with the RAF, was posted missing, believed dead.

Little sport was played but on Boxing Day, 1939 Halstead Town entertained and beat the Old Colonians 6-3.

Halstead: C. Barnes, A. Osborne, T. Barron, J. Edwards, E. Webber, G. Cutmore, D. Newton, J. Curtis, J. Webber, W. Edwards and E. Harper.

Old Colonians: J. Borrett, J. Reynolds, T. Rice, J. Rippingale, F. Rayner, F. Hostler, P. Griffiths, F. Squirrell, R. Joyce, L. Dean and G. Pudney.

To round off the year parties for the children were held at the Queens Hall, Trinity Parish Room, the Co-op Hall and Imps Hall in Head Street as well as many village halls.

HALSTEAD RURAL DISTRICT COUNCIL.

CORNFIELD FIRE FIGHTING.

In addition to the Council's Fire Service of a medium Trailer Pump at Earls Colne and Great Yeldham and auxiliary light Trailer Pumps at Sible Hedingham and Foxearth, the Council have also issued especially for Cornfield Fires a light Trailer Pump at Greenstead Green and at Steeple Bumpstead. Manual and Stirrup Pumps have also been issued throughout the district.

All Farmers and rural residents are urged to co-operate in this scheme as follows :—

By making available and marking water supplies, such as ponds, streams, etc.

By keeping all Water Carts filled and ready to move with towing vehicles if possible.

By making known and volunteering to assist with the local Trailer Pump Team or Manual and Stirrup Pump Parties.

G. F. DEARMAN,
Supt. of Rural Fire Brigades.

Rural Council Offices,
Colchester Road,
Halstead, Essex.

6

Residents of Halstead were able to look at the war from afar so to speak when both picture houses, The Empire and the Colne Valley Cinema showed the film 'The Lion has Wings'. This was the story of the RAF raid on Kiel, but the wartime censor had obviously used his 'blue pencil' to good effect!

Germany's threat of large scale air attacks on Great Britain did not materialise. This may have been because of political or economic reasons, although it was probably through fear of reprisals.

By February the number of evacuees in the area had dropped tremendously said the HUDC, with some two thirds of them having gone home leaving only about 400 or less. But the spirit of the local populace was not to be dimmed, for they kept a smile on their faces by staging a variety of shows, one in particular at St. Andrews Hall, which was in aid of the ARP (Shades of Dad's Army!)

Despite the importance of a little thing called the Second World War, bureaucracy would not be moved.

A letter published in the Halstead Gazette from a Mr. F.C. Krailing, of Stambourne, revealed: 'Wanting some paraffin, which will not be sent unless cash is sent in advance, although I have been a customer for many years. I wanted a postal order for 15/5d, but they were out of 15/- orders and gave my messenger one for 14/-, with a 5d stamp thereon and six 2ds totalling 15/5d. In turn I received a note with the 15/5d saying — The Petroleum Board have not the facilities for disposing of stamps, please send a 15/5d postal order. No wonder the Control Offices require such enormous staffs."

In an effort to save electricity Double Summer Time was introduced in February thus allowing longer working hours for the population who did not need power for their labours. I remember playing football at Kings Road playing field when my parents turned up 10.40 p.m. "Oi', It's time you were home young man!"

The UDC's early billetting office in Halstead, formerly known as Hedingham Radio (Harvey's in Hedingham Road) closed down and facilities were switched to Red House where provisions were made to accept more evacuees to the area, the quota for the Urban being 300, with 1,000 in the Rural district, 10/6d per week allowed for under 14s.

The hostilities led to Halstead Town Football Club closing down as they were unable to carry on with most of their players away serving King and Country. Being unable to pay its way the club were forced to give up the use of the ground in Kings Road (Ravens Meadow) and offered the stand and pavilion for sale.

Warnings were issued to the population not to stand and stare up at the sky during an air raid. A person should get under cover, for a 500lb high explosive bomb dropping within 50 yards of its target will flatten everything in that radius; a 250 pounder does likewise within 15 yards. If there is no cover a person was advised to lay flat on their backs in a dry ditch. There was no mention if it was a wet one!

One good piece of news was the meeting in Canada of Great Yeldham brothers, Maurice and Bert Abrahams, the former having emigrated some years earlier, the latter subsequently posted to the Dominion with the RAF.

By the end of March Halstead ARP could boast their own social club at Nether Priors in Colchester Road, where many a local warden could recall a wartime tale.

Soon after the declaration of war a Hospital Supply Depot was set up in Halstead, a house called Eastdene, on the corner of Trinity and New Streets, opposite the present council offices, where splendid work was carried out by Mrs Francis Adams with Mrs Hicks as her deputy. Whist drives as part of fund raising ventures were common as were knitting parties. The ladies were doing their bit by 'Knitting for Victory', following the men's cry 'Dig for Victory' thus making people as self sufficient as possible. These activities were carried out throughout the length and breadth of the land, in village hall, private houses and in public halls.

At the meeting of the HRDC members heard that under new Government regulations regarding billeting of evacuees, some form of compulsory purchase may be necessary with a number of houses standing empty in the area.

There were 33 new inmates at Gosfield Hall while the people of Birdbrook complained of their inability to house any evacuees owing to the fact they had to walk half a mile to obtain their water from a pump in Moat Road. At Great and Little Yeldham it was suggested that 1,000 could be accommodated in empty Land Settlement houses.

The then Minister of Health, Walter Elliott, made a plea to the nation through the postbox to search their hearts to find room for unfortunate children who were bombed out, and a roll of facilities would be drawn up in every town and village.

With food now on ration many petty squabbles broke out. It must be remembered that it was necessary to register with a retailer for goods, which could not be obtained in other shops offering the same goods. In one case a grocer was not registered with the butcher for meat, and consequently the butcher wished to transfer his grocery coupons, a far cry from today when people have unlimited choice.

Over 70,000 coupons were used weekly in the area and all had to come through the Food Office and all had to be checked. The chairman of this committee, who shall remain nameless said "For goodness sake, let's not have any more officials to count coupons!"

The clerk of HUDC, Ronald Long, reported that nearly four tons of sugar was available to make marmalade, that constituted 862 coupons. He further outlined that certain amounts of 'Ration Free' sugar had been issued, explaining that sugar was ruined by a burst pipe at Stanley Symonds', in Bridge Street (on site of Wimpy Bar), and replacement was necessary for damaged bacon and ham at the Home and Colonial in Trinity Street (now Hannah's Kitchen). Other sugar was spoiled at the International Stores in the High Street (now Curry's).

The Food Committee further agreed that extra sugar should be made available for people wishing to make jam from soft fruit they grew themselves.

Mr. Dearman the local Fuel Officer was asked by the council to explain the shortages of coal in the district, and he replied that he intended to communicate with the Minister of Mines to ascertain when deliveries will take place!

The Welfare Committee were told at their weekly meeting that Miss Vaizey had resigned after reporting that there had been not much demand for her services, there being little call for clothing and none at all for boots. This left Mrs. Billett, Mrs. Norman, Mrs. Joyce, Mrs. Hughes and Mrs. Harris. In the meantime the sewing section was still busy at Eastdene, New Street.

In April the former manager of the Plaza Cinema at Sible Hedingham took up an appointment to take variety parties out to France to entertain the troops.

Halstead received a pat on the back from the organisers of National Savings Week, the local secretary announcing that £10,000 had been raised in a week following the government's appeal 'Lend to Defend'. Included in 44 savings associations in the Colne Valley were: Halstead Council School — £119; Girls Grammar School — £60; Castle Hedingham WI — £400 while the county town of Chelmsford raised £1,000.

A Wakes Colne man, P/Off J.A. Friend was Killed in Action with the RAF.

With the withdrawal of the Allied Expeditionary Force from France, several local men being picked off the beaches at Dunkirk, the nation was warned of the possible increase in hostilities and were encouraged to prepare air raid shelters and trenches,

although many of the former had already been completed.

This point was raised at the UDC meeting, when the clerk, Ronald Long informed the chairman Ted Parker, that about 70 parties of three or four would be enough to man stirrup pump parties in the town, Sid Pole suggested that a shelter large enough for 100 people should be erected in the High Street, while in the meantime the RDC heard of the prompt work of the Great Yeldham fire brigade who dealt with a fire at Baythorn Hall, under their captain, Carleton Whitlock.

In June it was announced that Italy had declared war on Great Britain and France, to which the Commonwealth countries promptly responded.

Following the proposal that communal shelters be built council members examined various cellars in the town and it was revealed that three were suitable: Mr. Yerbury, 28 Head Street; Baylis, 9 High Street and The Manse, in High Street, site of the present Post Office.

To prevent the waste of surplus fruit in country districts, Surplus Fruit Disposal Committees (!) were set up at the instigation of the Minister of Food, and the local horticultural societies, Womens Institutes, Red Cross Associations and WVS were asked to take part in organising the move.

A grand jam making session took place at the Technical School, Bridge Street (now public library) where in two days 575lbs of fruit was received, mostly plums. This eventually was turned into 500 lbs of jam by many volunteers, among them six being affectionately known as 'The Jam Tarts', which included Mrs. Morgan Hughes, Miss Wendy Gosling, Miss Ann Gray, Mrs. Grey and Miss Flower. The Food Committee responded by thanking all concerned including Mr. F. A. Last of the local gas company for providing the appliances for cooking.

The suggestion that Halstead cinemas be opened on a Sunday caused great consternation in parts of the town, some people complaining at the idea with their opponents pointing out if pubs were open all the week, there was nothing wrong in cinemas being open. In the end the town council was called in to sort the problem out and it was agreed by six votes to five to allow cinemas to be open on Sundays stipulating no admittance to under 14 year olds, and that films should be of a religious or uplifting nature.

In July, Ron Rayner of Head Street, Halstead was reported KIA.

As could well be imagined, back in the war years and the blackouts, it was inevitable that some people would find themselves in court for permitting a light to be seen. One such case involved no less a person than Captain Evan Hemming, CO of the Halstead, Braintree and Witham ARP! ! !

On 26th August, the first German aircraft crashed in the area, a Messerschmitt 110 at Burtons Green. A farm worker saw the 110 attacked by a British fighter and sparks began to appear, which increased to smoke and flames as it crashed into a field of clover, the two engines being thrown clear of the aircraft. The two crewmen's bodies were taken from the wreckage. Both were wearing the Iron Cross.

A few miles away at Colne Engaine, a Spitfire Fund was launched at a public meeting in the village hall, where Sir James Adam, CBE, KC, JP, of Colne Park presided, and £120 was promised by residents.

The following week a similar fund was set up in Halstead by the chairman of the council, Charlie Ready, who announced the cost of aircraft as: Spitfire-£6,000; Hurricane-£4,500; Blenheim-£17,000;Wellington-£25,000 and Sunderland-£50,000.

On the last day of August a Heinkel 111 came down at Peveralls Farm, Colne Engaine at about 17.40 hrs. It had been attacked by British fighters and was seen to cover several miles in a steady glide coming down in a belly landing watched by 12 year old Joe Barnes sitting on his back door step. It had a crew of five, one was killed, three wounded and the other unhurt. One of the first men on the scene was a retired policeman, who incidentally belonged to the Red Cross, and another resident was out complete with shotgun, in search of a dinner, with which he conveniently apprehended the Germans until the autorities could be summoned.

The dead man was Oberfeldwebel Thomas Deitrich, of Tunkefeld, who was buried at Halstead Cemetery with full military honours after a service at the Roman Catholic church. His remains were exhumed and re-buried in Germany some thirty years later.

On behalf of Halstead Fighter Fund, Halstead Cricket Club took on an Army XI at Star Stile. It was a cold, grey day, when the Army batted first making 113, John Reynolds taking 4-41 and Harry Clark 4-50. In reply Halstead reached their target with seven wickets to spare, opener Bob Joyce making 46 and F.Sgt G. Unwin 32.

In the meantime a number of other fighter funds had been put into operation by many villages, and after three weeks, Halstead's fund had reached £247/2/6d.

AC Mortyn Downing of Gosfield was WIA with RAF, and Dvr Lance Dixey of Pebmarsh was taken POW.

A German bomber kindly left an unexploded bomb in Oak Road, Halstead on the night of 9th October, close to the edge of the field, almost exactly opposite Oak House, and for many years the hole was a pond. I can remember going up to have a look with a couple of school mates but we were not allowed near it, for the road was closed for several weeks while the bomb disposal experts went to work.

An attempt at German propaganda did not quite work out on 14th October when a partly deflated balloon was found at Birdbrook, with a box about a foot square on the end of a line. It was brought to Halstead police station about noon when a clockwork mechanism began and with a flash leaflets popped out.

They contained a photograph of Winston Churchill with the suggestion he be indicted for murder. A policeman was slightly scorched and his hair singed but he obtained no serious injury, although he was relieved of duty for the rest of the day on medical advice.

Remembrance Day 1940 was celebrated as usual, the service being conducted by Canon T. H. Curling, assisted by the local British Legion chaplain Rev. C. H. M. Fasson, of Greenstead Green. The parade was under Captain W. A. Nicholson, president of the local Legion branch.

Members of the first aid section of the ARP took umbrage over press reports that high quality food was being supplied to those on duty, such as eggs and bacon. Their reply was 'Never at any time have we had anything more luxurious than bread and cheese; usually in peace time this was considered a tramp's ration'.

An exhibition of model aircraft was staged in the Baptist Schoolroom in Hedingham Road, by the Model Aero Club. On display were an ME109 by Mr. C Rowland; Hawker Hurricane by Master D. Fisher; Boulton Paul Defiant by Mr. P. Hewitt; Vickers Wellington by Mr. F. J. Mitson, while Cyril Smith of Sible Hedingham had drawings of the interior of a Dornier 125 on show. The president of the club was Rev. D. V. Barber, secretary David Harvey, both assisted by Miss C. Le Meseurier.

A large cellar belonging to the Adams family in Trinity Street, Halstead was to be made available for another air raid shelter. The house is now the Council Offices.

Sgt Ken Ridgewell of Halstead was repatriated after being MIA with the

RAF.

A meeting was called in the High Street Chapel Hall, Halstead, to discuss the possibility of providing entertainment for the many evacuees in the town. A committee was formed from the attendance of over 100 and the first thing agreed was to find facilities for communal feeding, such as a restaurant, chairman Charlie Ready estimating the cost of such meals would be 8d for adults and 4d for children.

By the end of the year Halsteads Fighter Fund had topped £880, and the town council were looking to reach the £1,000 mark as soon as possible. As part of the fund raising activities there was an exhibition with a difference, when a German ME109 was put on display in the Co-operative Society's Garage in Bridge Street, with a competition for guessing the weight — adults 6d and children 3d. However it appears that no correct answer was forthcoming from any of the 1,300 that attended throughout the week.

Early in the year Halstead Choral Society was asked to assist in a BBC radio broadcast, the male quintet consisting of Stanley Britton, Bob Potts, Hurrell Rayner, Stanley Symonds and R.D. Fisher, took part in a programme called 'They went with it'.

A clothing depot for evacuees was opened at 15 Head Street, Halstead where the WVS were present on Monday, Wednesday and Friday afternoons.

The ARP issued a public warning that a considerable number of incendiary bombs may have been dropped in the area, and in the event the Air Raid Wardens would 'Sound short, sharp blasts on their whistles'.

Halstead Food Committee was still busy organising the disposal of surplus fruit and reported that the depot at the Technical School had processed 7,000 lbs of jam all of which was of 'An excellent quality'. Reference was made to the communal feeding of evacuees it being pointed out that the only facilities suitable were the canteen at Courtaulds and the dining room at the Council School, but following a request for help in the local press, only four people had volunteered to assist.

By the end of January Halstead's Fighter Fund reached the magical four figure target of £1,000, which included 16/6d from the sale of three oil paintings, by Mr G. Carter at an ARP dance!

At Nether Priors, the HQ of the ARP, there were grumblings about personnel having worked many months without a holiday, and because a tender of £4/10/- had been accepted for the decoration of the kitchen by Walter Lee, of Crowbridge.

In early February the Halstead Air Training Corps were formed, with recruiting centres at Halstead, Earls Colne and Sible Hedingham. It was hoped to have squadrons formed of about 50 boys who would undergo various types of training and would be issued with a uniform similar to the RAF. These centres were set up under Messrs H. W. Frost, J. G. Sykes and R. L. Baker at the three schools.

Dig for Victory plans were issued by the government, and the town council heard several plots had been taken up at Mitchell Avenue and Windmill Field (Road), with only about a dozen plots vacant. Horticultural advice was issued for publication, all national and local newspaper pointing out that any little odd corner of land could produce something.

A total of 71 youngsters enrolled to join the newly formed Air Training Cadets as it was called, and after considerable study by the committee it was agreed that Earls Colne Grammar School was the most suitable venue for the squadron, being called No. 1163 Colne Valley Squadron, the C.O. being Ronald Long.

Training sessions were held all over the town and district for members of the ARP, Red Cross, Fire Brigade to make sure each individual knew what to do in the event of an air raid, and how precautions would go a long way towards the well-being of the populace. A list of points where ladders and stirrup pumps were to be found was issued to all.

Shelters were set up for fire bomb

watchers at the top of Mitchell Avenue with the junctions and Ramsey Road and Holman Road; Moy's Office in Kings Road; Warden's post on Tidings Hill and Sidney Tomlinson's shed in Balls Chase to name but a few.

Essex County Council issued a circular pointing out the dangers in contaminated clothing and Capt Hemming of the ARP visited St Mary's Home, Great Maplestead to see if the facilities there could be made available in an emergency.

An application for another siren in Halstead was turned down by the County Council, despite the plea by Francis Adams that the present siren at the police station could not be heard at the Kings Head in Colchester Road, there were four or five sirens in Braintree.

At the annual meeting of HUDC Harry Sturmer was elected as the new chairman in place of Charlie Ready.

Capt Guy Ruggles-Brise of Spains Hall, Finchingfield was MIA.

Speaking at Dunmow, the Rt. Hon. R.A. Butler said he found it difficult to understand why Rudolf Hess had arrived in England, how he did so, especially someone so closely associated with Hitler but hoped he would be treated no better or worse than any other prisoner of war.

On Whit Monday 1941 Halstead took on the RAF at cricket at Star Stile. The visitors were all out for 92, Cyril Evans taking 6-28 then went on to top score with 33, the Town won with wickets to spare.

With nearly two years of the war having passed, Halstead was now well prepared for air raids and the town council issued a list of shelters for the residents use in an emergency.

Viz.: John Watkinson, 100 Mount Pleasant; Fred Bragg, The Hole, Mount Pleasant; Jack Osborne, 52 Mount Pleasant (I helped dig this one !!!) Mr C Barrett, 11 New Street; Mr Ellis, 14 New Street; John Abraham, 46 New Street; Mrs Reynolds, 13 Brook Place; Mr W. Clements, 33 Trinity Square (now Butler Road); Wally Pilgrim, Chapel Street; Aubrey Porter, Chapel Street, corner of tannery; Harry Hughes, Westbourne, Chapel Street; Mr G. Graham, Belle Vue Terrace; Stan Gladwell, Belle Vue Terrace, north end; Mr J. Flatt, Mill Chase, Hedingham Road; Mr G. Wishart, 1 School Lane, Head Street; no occupier, south west corner of Bois Farm, Colne Road; Mr. P.E. Root, 38 Head Street; Mr E. Claydon, Rose Yard, Head Street; no occupier, 19 Mount Hill; Percy Brazier, 8 Chapel Hill; Fred Smith, 5 Trinity Terrace; Arthur Coote, north of chase, Trinity Road; Mr H. Harrington, 49 Trinity Road; Mr W Sayward, 42 Trinity Road; Len Rose, 19 Trinity Road; Mr A. Smith, 20 Trinity Road and Ron Parr, Upper Trinity Road; Appointed superintendents were: Aubrey Sayward, Ben Paveley, Joe Jackson and Alf Snowden.

Halstead decided to have a War Weapons Week setting a target of £50,000, to be raised from different functions, July 19-26. It kicked off with a procession of local institutions which marched from Pretoria Road to the Public Gardens. Throughout the week there were whist drives, dances, bowls competitions, boxing tournaments, dancing displays, girl guides, cricket matches, exhibitions and displays by the Red Cross, Fire Brigade, Home Guard and a special film at The Cinema each day.

14

The target of £50,000 was easily beaten on the first day, with all the local villages co-operating with their own activities and at the end of a tremendous week the magnificent sum of £276,334/3/6d was raised, over a quarter of a million pounds. No wonder there were tumultuous cheers when this was announced from the fountain on Halstead's Market Hill. The town subsequently received written thanks from the then Chancellor of the Exchequer, Sir Kingsley Wood.

Halsteadians were kept well up to date with the latest technical advances of allied aircraft, with regular columns describing details of range, speed climbing heights, etc., presumably in the knowledge that the Axis already knew!

The question of fish and chips was raised at a meeting of HUDC, members hearing complaints that some retailers in the district were refusing to sell chips without fish. Now fish and chips being particularly British, the chairman pointed out that potatoes were the staple food of the country, and many people just could not afford to buy the fish, and he stressed it was illegal for retailers to impose such a condition on his customers.

"If he had chips, he should sell chips", said Charlie Ready, a former chairman.

The Fire Brigade was also discuseed and it was announced that the town was to have it first full time fireman, a Ronald Tyrell, his hours being 10am-10pm. He would be responsible for maintaining the equipment in good order. Older local residents might remember Ron Tyrell as mine host at the Nags Head, Halstead, who later moved to the Freemasons Arms, Braintree.

It was reported that 2nd Ltd Basil Francis of Beards, Great Yeldham was taken POW.

Months previously concern had been expressed about the inability of the authorities to provide common feeding facilities, especially for the evacuees. A solution to the problem arrived with the purchase of a former butcher's shop in Trinity Street, Halstead, formerly belonging to Ted Doe who had just retired. It was to be known as 'The British Restaurant', and stood on the empty ground next to the current Tristar Motor Cycle shop.

I well remember this myself, it being of two floors, with three dining rooms, the fourth room, on the right on entering, was the cooking area. The cashier was a Mrs Coe who counted up as the customers collected the food from the servers.

Despite the war Halsteadians carried on as normal, at least as far as they could, going to work and about their daily business as well as finding time to relax, the many clubs and institutions providing this outlet.

In September the latest organisation to spring up was the 1st Halstead Life Boys, when enrolments took place at the Council School hall. Under Rev. G. W. Kirby, of the New Congregational Church, some 30 boys signed up. They were taught various crafts in the church hall on Monday evenings by Mrs Hermon, Mrs Howe and Mrs Overall. In later years, a similar organisation, the Boys Brigade, were remembered for their band and marches around the streets of the town on Sunday mornings.

It was reported Pte Les Brett, of Swan Street, Sible Hedingham was KIA.

In an effort to maintain the flow of

materials, the Ministry of Supply contacted all local authorities throughout the land with the view to obtaining more iron and steel from fence railings, and the HUDC responded by offering the fence around the Public Gardens. The Rural District added that there were plenty of small railings surrounding monuments in churchyards, numerous lamp posts and other unnecessary fences in the town. About 60 tons were collected.

The Halstead Industrial Co-operative Society houses in Trinity Road and Mitchell Avenue were shorn of cast iron fences, although the gates still remain, in most cases with HICS 1891 (or whatever date) as originally cast. Similar fences came down in Beridge Road and Stanley Road.

Some railings still stand at the Public Gardens, in Kings Road and New Street, outside the Community Centre, as well as the four gates.

Showing at Halstead Empire in early October was the film 'Target for Tonight', about a raid on Germany. The press described it as 'Amazing', 'Stupendous', 'The real thing'.

After the tremendous response for War Weapons Week in Halstead a campaign was launched for Warship Week with a target of £10 per head, which raised £60,000 in the urban and £160,000 in the rural districts, while in the meantime the YMCA appeal had reached over £524.

Another fund raising exercise was called 'Help for Russia Fund'. Little did the organisers of the National Council for Labour realise how things were to change! It met with little response, for by the end of the year the fund had failed to reach three figures.

The War Office announced Sgt J.C. Addy (RAF) was awarded the DFM (he lived at Blue Bridge, Halstead). Gnr Thomas Pilgrim, of Colne Road, Halstead was KIA.

HALSTEAD & DISTRICT
War Weapons Week
Halstead's Programme of Activities.

SATURDAY, July 19th.—MILITARY and CIVIL PROCESSION with Military Band, Pipers. Tableaux, etc., starting from Pretoria Road at **6.30 p.m.,** proceeding by High Street to Public Gardens.

Inspection and Opening Speeches in Public Gardens by **SIR RONALD STORRS, K.C.M.G., C.B.E., LL.D.,** and the **RT. HON. R. A. BUTLER, M.P.**

Selections by Military Band.

Tennis Tournament (Mixed Doubles, enter with partner). Entries to Mr. G. Preece, Sudbury Road, Halstead; or Mr. S. R. Britton, Colchester Road. Halstead. Entry Fee **4/-** per couple.

SUNDAY, July 20th.—CRUSADE SERVICE in Churches.

MONDAY, July 21st.—Announcement of Grand Total at 12.15 p.m. each day at Fountain, Market Hill.

7.0 p.m. WHIST DRIVE in Co-operative Hall. Admission **1/-**.

8 to 12 p.m. DANCE in the newly-decorated Queens Hall by **Royal Corps of Signals.** Entire proceeds, free of all expenses, to be given to the Halstead Hospital Children's Ward Investment Fund in Government Bonds through the Halstead War Weapons Week. Tickets **2/-**. Novelty Competitions and Prizes.

TUESDAY, July 22nd.—7.0 p.m. SCOUT DISPLAY by Pupils of Gosfield School in St. Andrew's Vicarage Gardens. Admission **3d.**

WEDNESDAY, July 23rd.—3.0 p.m. PARTNER BRIDGE DRIVE in Co-operative Hall. Admission **1/6.**

8.0 p.m. to 1.0 a.m. POPULAR DANCE in Co-operative Hall, arranged by Mr. F. A. Warren. Admission **2/6.**

THURSDAY, July 24th.—7.0 p.m. MUSICAL DRILL, COUNTRY DANCES, P.T., BOXING and SINGING by Halstead Council School. Admission **6d.** Children **3d.**

8.15 p.m. DISPLAY by Fire Brigade and A.R.P. Both in the Public Gardens.

FRIDAY, July 25th.—7.0 p.m. GIRL GUIDE DISPLAY in Children's Playing Field, School Chase. Admission **3d.**

9.0 p.m. to 2.0 a.m. GRAND DANCE in the newly-decorated Queens Hall by **Royal Corps of Signals.** The entire proceeds, free of all expenses, to be given to the Halstead Hospital Children's Ward Investment Fund in Government Bonds through the Halstead War Weapons Week. Novelty Competitions and Prizes. Tickets **4/-**.

SATURDAY, July 26th.—2.30 p.m. CRICKET MATCH: Halstead v. R.A.S.C. on Sudbury Road Ground. Collection.

7.0 p.m. GRAND CONCERT in the Public Gardens, followed by **DANCING** on the Lawn. Admission **6d.** Children **3d.** DANCING **6d.**

SPECIAL FILM in Cinemas each day.

EXHIBITIONS in King George's Playing Field, Kings Road, and Showrooms of EAST ANGLIAN ELECTRIC SUPPLY CO. and the HALSTEAD GAS CO, LTD.

The Urban District Council were involved in most of the administration of Halstead at this time, and several appointments were made by this august body, for early in the year, Mrs L. Edwards was appointed cook-manageress at the British Restaurant, shortly to be opened, with Mrs W.H. Matthews as her assistant. Two other ladies were Mrs R. Sudbury and Mrs F. Shelley, who were on duty when the establishment opened on 18 February, when the local dignitaries had their usual free meal!

In February the Empire staged a Deanna Durbin Week, which in turn was part of Warship Week, and a Wastepaper Scheme was also launched. The villages too, joined in and each staged their own festivities and competitions.

Sgt Reg Bult (RAF), of Recreation Road, Sible Hedingham was KIA, and F/O Edward Schofield (RAF), of Colne Engaine was posted as missing. Eric Barwood, of Parsonage Street, Halstead was KIA with the Royal Navy.

Halstead Co-operative Society announced that bread deliveries would only be on alternate days in various streets, and within days other retailers followed suit after a special meeting in the Co-op Hall.

The Urban District Council announced they had received over 450 applications for Anderson and Morrison shelters, but pointed out the latter were not suitable for bungalows or houses of lath and plaster.

The town and surrounding villages responded to Warship Week with a magnificent total of £162,660, but the ARP were not so fortunate with their appeal for members when they had only four affirmative replies from over 400 letters sent out to form rescue parties in the event of an emergency.

In the middle of March Captain W.A. Nicholson stood down after 37 years with the local fire service, joining in 1904 when it was the Volunteer Brigade, which in turn was taken over by the HUDC, before becoming the Auxiliary, then National Fire Service.

In April seven Steeple Bumpstead men were listed as missing in action, who were all in the Suffolk Regiment which was overrun when Singapore capitulated. Several other men were also lost, but later listed as being Japanese POWs in the infamous Changi Jail.

Meantime the Essex Regiment containing more local men was serving in Tobruk and played a key part in the attack on El Duda. The desert conditions were terrible for them, with drinking water rationed, 50 cigarettes per week and seldom any beer. Digging trenches proved virtually impossible for they often had to negotiate enemy minefields as they gradually won back territory. Poor old Tommy!

At the meeting of the UDC it was recommended licences be granted for the storage of petrol to: Halstead Motor Co. Ltd. for 1,300 gallons; Eastern National Bus Co. for 2,000; and it was noted that petrol was stored at Messrs Chaplin & Keeble in the High Street and Messrs R. E. Coote & Son, at Mount Hill, for the use of different services controlled by the council. It was also agreed that the St Andrews church clock be allowed to chime again during the hours of daylight.

The RDC played its part in the collection of salvage with scrap metal being collected from Unwin's at Baythorne End; Mr C. Nott, Twinstead; George Courtauld, Colne Engaine, and bones being stored at Hedingham, where it was described that they were suspended in a wire cage out of the reach of dogs. Col. Sparrow stressing if they were boiled for soup first there would be no smell to attract dogs!

Following the success of the British Restaurant in Halstead, the village of Earls Colne pursued a similar venture, but the RDC were informed by the Minister of Food that the ministry would not supply accommodation or allow local authorities to build same. However the ministry offered several surplus War Department Nissen huts.

In June the ARP committee met at Nethers Priors when it was announced that Officer Mr W.P. Tyrell had been promoted and was to take up a post in London. His place was taken by the assistant county officer for training, Albert Bright, who eventually became landlord at the Carpenters Arms, Halstead.

Other personnel included: Sgt Redvers Simmons in charge of the rescue party; Sgt George Coe first aid; Cpl Reg Wishart, the deputy leader of the rescue party, with Cpl J.W. Cawston at Earls Colne. First aid party leaders were Jack Root and Bert Eley, for Halstead; L. Moss, Earls Colne; Reg Matthews, Colne Engaine and Cyril Smith, Sible Hedingham.

If it had not been so serious it would have been laughable, when a Hatfield Peverel man was taken to court because he had a bonfire blazing merrily at night. The ARP were called out by complaints from a neighbour, but the culprit refused to get up when his door was knocked on. The Home Guard eventually extinguished the fire and the man was fined £5 and 14/9d costs!

Throughout the summer of 1942 people tried to live their lives as normal as possible and villages continued to stage their annual fetes and flower shows despite the war.

That same summer was also very significant in that as Britain was in the process of defending herself against the Hun, she was taking steps to go on the offensive with the building of many airfields, especially in East Anglia, with the American Eighth Air Force having moved to England.

Three were built in the immediate district and by the autumn Earls Colne, Gosfield and Ridgewell were ready for action although they did not become operational immediately.

The latter was a typical field built for the heavy bombers of the American Army Air Force, the B17 Flying Fortresses. Some 1,170,000 man hours were needed for its construction and no less than a million cubic yards of concrete were used sufficient for 45 miles of standard two lane highways. Six miles of 4" and 6" water mains were laid, 12 miles of French drains, seven miles of storm drains and five miles of foul drainage. On the site were more than 500 buildings and a sewerage plant to handle a population of 2,500.

The Royal Air Force were actually first in at Ridgewell when No.90 Squadron moved in under Wing Co Charles Dawson, flying Short Stirlings.

Over at Gosfield young Albert Cross, a private in the Royal Signal Corps was on duty at the Hall, which was being used as troop billets when up rumbled a US Army Construction Battn in the middle of the night. "We've come to build an airfield" was the reply when challenged! Later Albert did duty at Sloe House, Halstead, a HQ of the Royal Signals where there was also a section of homing pigeons used for communications.

In April several local men were reported as missing or killed: Cpl Edward Harrison, and brother Norman, both of Mill House, Steeple Bumpstead and Pte Reg Wesley of The Stores in the same village who was KIA, as was Cpl Arthur Parish of Little Maplestead. Others reported during the next few weeks were: Gnr Bill Edwards, Colchester Road: Gnr Tom Beckwith, Mount Pleasant; Pte Percy Constable, Windmill Road; Pte J.W. Jarman, Colne Road, all Halstead, were taken POW, while Sgt Vic Banbury, High Street, Halstead was KIA; Others missing were Pte Sonny Pilgrim, Gosfield; Pte Bernard Gillbanks, Three Tuns, Finchingfield; brothers Bob and Alfred Harding of Mill Farm, Steeple Bumpstead; Bdr Tom Lowery, Tilbury Road and Pte Jack Alliston, Poole Street, both Great Yeldham.

In May: Pte A.J. Higgleton, Coggeshall Road, Earls Colne and Pte George Backler, Blois Road, Steeple Bumpstead; in June: Lt A.F. Hall, of Applegates, Great Yeldham.

During July RN Comdr Geoffrey Gibson, of Stones Grange, Halstead was awarded the OBE by King George VI. Posted missing were: Gnr S. Reynolds, Colne Park Road, Colne Engaine; Sgt Neville Chumbley, Ramsey Road; Pte Ken Hart, Head Street; Pte John Bullard, West Road; Sgt Bert Bragg, Harvey Street; Pte Fred Coe, Harvey Street; Pte Reg Cook, Fenn Road, all Halstead; Spr Reg Rose, Grove Cottage, Sible Hedingham; Sgt Fred Carter, Council Houses, Colne Engaine; Sgn Wilf Clark, Colne Ford Hill, White Colne; Pte Alf Cousins, Mill Lane Pebmarsh; Pte Harold Earey, Potter Street, Sible Hedingham and Gnr Albert Reeve, Council Houses, Gestingthorpe.

Killed in action the same month were: Bdr Len Nunn, Trinity Road, and L/Bdr Mark Kibble, of Prospect Place, New Street, both Halstead; and P/Off. Derek Wales, of Windyridge, Finchingfield was wounded with the RAF.

Missing in action in August were; Pte John Eldred, Mallows Field; Cpl Dennis Lee, Colchester Road; Sgt Albie Smith, Factory Terrace, all Halstead; CQMS Bill Howe Langthorn Cottage, Little Maplestead.

Taken POW were: Sgt Maj Alf Jeggo, and brother John of Pink House, Great Maplestead; Spr Dennis Dowsett, Church Green, Castle Hedingham; Pte Arthur Simmons, School Road, Pte Edgar Wiseman, Egypt Cottages, both Little Maplestead; Pte Don Cutmore, Hyde Green, Blackmore End; CQMS Bill Williams, Gosfield; Spr Phillip Smith, North End, Little Yeldham; Pfc Roy Giller, Mallows Field; Cpl Bernard Hunt, Belle Vue; Pte Ted Mortimer, Fenn Road; Pte Harold Lock, Kings Road; S/Sgt Fred Patmore, Windmill Road; all Halstead.

By the end of the year P/O Robert (Bob) Sargent, of Hedingham Road, Halstead was missing with RAF, while his brother Bill and A/B Leslie Gibson, Ridgewell Road, Gt. Yeldham were both KIA with the Royal Navy.

The year opened with the War Department announcing that Sgt Cliff Sudbury of Stanley Road, Halstead was taken POW and that P/O John Butler, was KIA with RAF. He was the younger brother of the Rt. Hon. Rab Butler, MP, of Stansted Hall.

In February the HUDC discussed the possibility of ploughing up part of the Public Gardens, with part being used as a hostel for American troops stationed in the area. The proposal to erect buildings for games, rest, reading and baths. These are now used as the Community Centre, in New Street, Halstead.

Such was the shortage of food in those days that even to sell biscuits a licence was needed, so found out the landlord of The Anchor, Halstead, and The Donkey at Ovington, who wished to provide bread and cheese. While at the same court, an RAF Sgt from Ridgewell was summoned for giving a lift to his girl friend on the cross bar of his bicycle. "The law must be upheld" said the magistrates!!!

Two Halstead brothers, Jack and John Curtis, of Mallows Field, met in the RAF in the Middle East.

Gnr Tom Beckwith, of Mount Pleasant, reported missing a year earlier was confirmed a Japanese POW. Also missing was RAF Cpl Basil Hockley, of Chapel Hill, Halstead and F/Sgt Ernie Vale, of Christmas Field, Sible Hedingham, who was aboard a RAF bomber that crashlanded on the Scilly Isles after returning from a raid.

In May Lt. Alan Frost of The Mill, Halstead reported POW in North Africa and Pte George Basford of Windmill Road; Pte Harold Meadows, both Halstead; Spr Dennis Dowsett, of Castle Hedingham, all confirmed POW of the Japanese.

A Wings for Victory Week was launched with a target of £120,000, the cost of three Stirling bombers. This took the form of many games and competitions, both in Halstead and the villages. The festivities began with a parade of local organisations which marched from Colchester Road to the Public Gardens, the salute being taken by Mr R. A. Butler MP near the Eastern National garage. The people of Halstead and district again responded in magnificent style with over £213,000, enough for five Stirlings instead of three. The town itself raised £102,436, including gifts from local banks, and even the tiny village of Ovington found £76.

Pte Harold Kemp of Slipe Cottage, Great Yeldham was reported taken POW in the Far East.

"One of the best squadrons I have ever seen" was the comment by Air Chief Marshall Sir W.G.H. Mitchell, when he inspected 1163 Squadron ATC.

By the end of May the RAF had moved out of Ridgewell and were replaced by the 381st Bomb Group of the American Army Air Force, who were to remain for the duration, the only heavy bomber group to do so in Essex, using B17 Flying Fortresses.

After only one mission tragedy hit the base in late June. For when the aircraft were being loaded for a mission, there was an accident, which led to a huge explosion resulting in the deaths of 24, including a civilian John Hunwick who was working nearby. The aircraft was completely destroyed and several others badly damaged.

The proposal to erect a hostel for the US forces was deferred by the UDC and there would be no objection if the site was ploughed up.

Two Halstead men met in Africa, Dvr Dick Byham of Hedingham Road, serving in the Royal Signals, met his next door neighbour Pte George Green, serving in the Essex Regiment. RAF W/O Suckling of Paynters Terrace, Halstead was mentioned in dispatches.

In July an artist 'of great repute' from Toppesfield offered to decorate the walls of the British Restaurant with pictures of flowers and landscapes, and true to the code of local government, the suggestion was taken up "providing it did not involve public spending," said the chairman of the day, Bert Lock.

Two Halstead men were reported Jap POWs; Ted Vitler, Chapel Hill; Bill Edwards, Tidings Hill, and Percy Peacock of Ashen; but Sgt Neville Chumbley of Ramsey Road, Halstead, was confirmed KIA a year earlier.

Mrs Winnie Metson (nee Goodwin), of the Causeway, Halstead was elected Halstead Holiday at Home Week beauty queen.

In September P/O Ken Turp, of Pretoria Road, Halstead was reported missing with the RAF, while an Italian POW was killed in a road accident at Penny Pots.

Two Halstead cousins met the following month, Cpl Harold Evans, Windmill Road, serving in the CMP and Cpl Wally May, of Manfield who was with the KRR. RAF Sgt Clifford Tarbin, of the Waggon & Horses, Great Yeldham and P/O Francis Beane of Ridgewell post office, were reported MIA.

At the October UDC meeting the council agreed to charge only a nominal sum per annum for the loss of the land in the Public Gardens to be used as an US forces hostel.

Lady Luba Fletcher, who was Russian born, and came to England after the Revolution, came to Halstead to talk on Life in Russia at the Co-op Hall under the auspices of the Minister of Information. The Communist party leader, Harry Pollitt came a few weeks later.

At the end of the month it was reported that two Castle Hedingham men had met in Palestine: LAC Rodney Hatfield (RAF) and L/Sgt Arthur Springett of Queens Street; Tpr Frank Mead of Chapel Hill, Halstead received severe burns, and Pte Henry Buckingham, of Wethersfield Road, Sible Hedingham, was missing; Gnr Richard Pakenham, of Coggeshall Road, Earls Colne was KIA, and Fred Picket of Pebmarsh Kings Head was awarded the British Empire Medal.

For a change there was traffic in the other direction when two former POWs were repatriated back to Halstead: CSM Leonard Watkin of Beridge Road and Pte Gordon Ince of High Street.

Concern was expressed by the HUDC over the amount of traffic in the town mostly of a military nature. Francis Adams reporting to the police that a US army vehicle in convoy mounted the pavement at Red House, Colchester Road. Also a complaint was received about children trespassing on the Mitchell Avenue allotments, and the parents were warned (So what else is new!!!)

In early November a new sound was heard on the streets of Halstead with the pleasant west country drawl of the 1st Battn Dorset Regiment, whose HQ was at Dynes Hall, the rest of the battalion being scattered in Halstead and surrounding villages.

Their stay was for only four months but they endeared themselves to the Halstead people, several ending up marrying local girls and settling in the town.

The two outstanding events during their stay was a visit by King George VI, with General Montgomery in attendance, to Dynes Hall to view a full scale crossing of the River Colne with full supporting arms.

Secondly, in February 1944, the whole regiment assembled at Ravens Meadow, in Kings Road, to be addressed by General Montgomery, who left the Dorsets in no doubt what their next task was to be; the assault on the second front.

It was with great reluctance the Dorsets left the friendliness of Halstead for the cold and bleak shores of Inverary, in Scotland.

However at the end of hostilities some returned to settle among the Halstead people including Arthur Kelson, Bill Petty, John Cribb, Alan Corben, Wally Lovesey, Bill Love, Douglas Strong, 'Paddy' Smythe, Harry Marshall and John Newport.

At one RAF station over a period of a few weeks, 1,300 ATC cadets working in shifts from early morning to late at night, even weekends and during the annual holidays, unloading and distributing 37 truckloads of bombs. They also belted and dispersed two million rounds of ammunition, salvaged tens of thousands of empty cases, helped to service, wash down and refuel aircraft and helped in many ways to speed the bombing offensive.

The station commander said it was difficult to get the cadets to stop working, they were so keen and there was not one case of bad discipline or slackness.

The chaplain at the US airfield at Ridgewell, Captain James Good Brown, gave a lecture at the Co-op Hall in early December on 'The American outlook on the world crisis'. The same Dr Brown returned in August 1982 to dedicate the memorial at the former base.

Five men listed as POWs were: Gnr Clifford Sudbury, of Stanley Road; Pte John Bullard, of West Road, both Halstead; Smn Wilf Clarke, Colne Ford Hill, White Colne; Pte Henry Buckingham, Wethersfield Road, Sible Hedingham and George Dennis of High Street, Great Yeldham: two posted MIA were Pte L.C. James, Parsonage Street and Pte Edward Willis, Belle Vue, both Halstead, in Singapore and Burma respectively.

Sixteen year old Arthur Bennett Hart, of Ramsey Road, Halstead, died from wounds received by bombs dropped by enemy aircraft over Box Mill, the only recorded death by military action in Halstead. He was hit by shrapnel and taken to Halstead Hospital for immediate treatment, thence to Black Notley where he died, apparently from infection.

Following the very successive Wings for Victory Week in Halstead and district, almost £138,000, enough for five Stirlings, was raised and the RAF presented a plaque to the chairman of the HRDC Robert Vaizey, and the log books of the aircraft in which the missions would be recorded for those alloted to the town. There was a similar presentation to Bert Lock of the UDC.

In December came the news that Sapper Dennis Cyril Dowsett of Castle Hedingham who was serving with the Royal Engineers had died on active war service on 2nd December. He was buried in Thanbyuzayat War Cemetery, Burma.

1944

At the first meeting of the year for HUDC, chairman Bert Lock pointed out to members that there were critical times ahead but if peace came early, the responsibilities of the council would increase when, as a result, we needed to make Halstead a better place to live in.

A record number of meals, 214, was served in a day at the British Restaurant in Trinity Street, said UDC clerk Ronald Long. At the same meeting it was announced a post war plan for 500 houses in the town with Nether Priors a possible site, however Harold Sturmer suggested Mitchell Avenue might be filled up first.

Rev. Frederick E. Bayley took over as vicar of Holy Trinity, on the retirement of Rev A.E. Austin.

News of local men serving in the forces revealed Gnr Jack Gardiner, of Colne Engaine was POW in Far East, while RAF Sgt Tom Finch of Fenn Road, Halstead was MIA. There was better news when Halstead men met overseas: Albert Chaplin (REME) of Tidings Hill and Kenneth Hunt serving in the RAF. Lewis Rollingson a RAF Sgt of High Street Green, Sible Hedingham was MIA, but RAF Sgts Frank Tempan of Mitchells Avenue Halstead and Cliff Tarbin, of Great Yeldham were KIA.

At the end of January the Anglo-American Club was opened in New Street near the Public Gardens. Although primarily for the use of the US Forces, it was available for the British, and Mr Z.F. Willis, the general secretary of the National Association of YMCAs hoped that all would take advantage of such a splen-did facility.

It had a main hall used as a canteen, smaller rooms for reading, cards, darts and other games as well as a billiard room. Among those at the opening ceremony was the Bishop of Chelmsford, UDC chairman Bert Lock, Samuel Courtauld (Essex Welfare Committee), Mr H.W. Palmer (American Red Cross) and Col J.E. Miller, representing the Chief of Staff, First Air Division, USAAF. The proceedings closed with the National Anthem and the Star Spangled Banner.

The resident staff were: Mrs Shepherd, Mr H.W. Moore and Mr Beckett and there were numerous voluntary helpers. I remember as a youngster along with others from the Mount Pleasant and Mitchell Avenue area, that there used to be dozens of bikes leaning against the fence and we used to borrow them to ride up and down New Street. We were not big enough to get on and ride properly, we used to put a leg under the cross bar and reach the pedals and nip up and down lopsided. There were plenty of crashes and grazes but no permanent damage!

The 'gang' as I recall included Mike Bush, 'Pop' Bearham, Colin Cook, Ray Cook, Melvy Draper, Russell Blogg and one or two girls if they were brave enough!

At their February meeting the HUDC were presented with a collection of paintings and drawings of Old Halstead by Morton Mathews a former headmaster of the Council School. Members were unanimous that they hang in the council chamber, and were extremely grateful. Members also heard that during the last quarter of 1943 the British Restaurant had supplied 11,453 cups of tea to the workers at Portways Foundry.

Basil Harvey of Newhouse Road, Earls Colne was KIA, while L/Cpl Fred Smith, of Bois Field Halstead was MIA.

Halstead Council School held a boxing tournament in the main hall in March, some of the results being: Donald Adams beat Keith Baker in the Cutting Cup final; House results: Cedric Pilgrim (Y) bt John Taylor (B); Terry Bragg (Y) bt Keith Kibble (G); Eric Cook (R) bt Fred Amos (B); Reg Smith (G) bt Ray Kirby (Y); Peter Mortimer (G) bt Bert Rulton (Y); Eric Smith (R) bt Philip Carter (R); John Barnes (Y) bt Bobby Letham (Y); and in other matches Guy (Colchester) bt Brian Rippingale and Ken Amos bt Christie (Colchester).

Salute the Soldier Week in Halstead was arranged as more National Savings were still required and it was announced that a private from the Essex Regiment will take the salute, the targets being £50,000 from the UDC and £100,000 from the RDC.

News of serving men: Pte Peter Flack, Upper Trinity Road, Halstead RAF Cpl Kenneth Cook of Greenstead Green and RAF Sgt Ron Smith of North End, Little Yeldham were all WIA.

Three Maplestead children were injured when they picked up an unusual object which turned out to be a hand grenade. They were Ivy Jeggo 9, Roy Jeggo 5 and Ronnie Clampin 7. They were taken and detained in Halstead Hospital with leg and lower body injuries.

A few miles away at Gestingthorpe tragedy struck when six men were killed during a Home Guard exercise, apparently when a grenade was being handled. The blast made a hole a foot deep, five feet long and two feet wide, at Rectory Farm.

Those who died were: Capt John Philp, of Rectory Farm; Sgt Tom Firman, Sgt Henry Cousins and Cpl Cyril Hall all of Sible Hedingham; Cpl George Chambers of Pentlow; Cpl John Partridge of Belchamp Walter. Three men were injured: Sgt Ken Wallace, of Great Maplestead (arm) and Sgt Fred Lock of Gosfield and Cpl Ernie Lott of Bulmer, both with eye injuries.

P/O Sidney Brooks of Burtons Green was KIA and Pte James Worlledge of Nunnery Street, Castle Hedingham was WIA in Burma.

Sidney Pole was elected chairman of HUDC, an enthusiastic worker for the 'Dig for Victory' campaign.

In May the new HQ of 1163 Squadron ATC was opened in Mallows Field, Halstead by Air Marshal Sir Leslie Gossage, from what was once a wireworkers workshop for Mr Brazier. The cadets paraded at full strength in Kings Rd under adjutant F/O W.A. Oakes and marched by way of Bridge Street and the High Street to Parsonage Street under bandmaster J.J. Smith. Several local dignitaries were present including Rt. Hon R.A. Butler, Ronald Long, Charlie Ready of the HUDC and representatives of the RAF and USAAF.

A Halstead soldier was picked for special duty when L/Cpl Eric Hardy of Ramsey Road, serving in CMP was detailed to the British Legation in Teheran when Winston Churchill was in conference. Four other Hardy brothers served: Pte Cyril in

Australian Imperial Forces; Sgmn Len and Pte Gerald in Essex Reg; Gnr Rex in Royal Artillery while two others Cpls Jack and Ted were in the Home Guard.

The Salute the Soldier Fund raised £128,712 in the HRDC and £70,935 in the UDC thus proving that Halstead and district will rally to the cause when required: War Weapons Week July 1941 — £276,334; Warship Week March 1942 — £162,661 and Wings for Victory Week, May 1943 — £213,409.

This made a grand total of £852,151.

News of local men serving: RAF Sgt Hedley Iron of Bois Field, Halstead was KIA; QMS Arthur Maskell of Parsonage Street, Halstead died in hospital in North Africa and Pte G. Mortimer of White Colne was WIA in Burma; RAF Sgt Jimmy Smith, Brookly, White Colne; Sgt George Louth, Tilbury Road, Great Yeldham and Pte John Chatters of Belchamp St Paul were all KIA. Wounded were Major R.B. Gosling, The Mote, Pebmarsh, Lt Percy Sneezum, Sudbury Road, Castle Hedingham; Dvr Leonard Bailey, Kings Road, Halstead; Sgt Arthur Kelson (Dorset Reg) who married a Halstead girl; Tpr John Saunders, Windmill Road, Pte Bob Taylor, Trinity Square; Pte Jackie Kensall, all Halstead, along with AC I Dennis Willingham, Croft Cottages, Earls Colne. Two men killed in action were RAF AC Duncan Brooks of Mitchell Avenue and Lt David Lowe, of Gosfield Hall.

In July Halstead Co-op celebrated 100 years of the movement with a fete in the Public Gardens (the local branch formed 1860), which included childrens sports, the Braintree Town Band giving selections, speeches and a play in the hall on Saturday and a concert on Sunday.

During the summer some 200 more evacuees had moved into the town but they had to find their own billets, the stream of visitors being unofficial and not organised by the UDC.

Pte Ken Hart of Head Street, Halstead, escaped as a POW. After being caught in Italy he was transferred to Germany, his fourth attempt being successful. It took him 14 months to make the journey.

Two Halstead brothers met in Normandy, Cpl Frank Wiffen, of Broomhills, Colchester Road, serving in RASC, met brother Tpr Donald (RAC); three others also served, one in India. Pte Les Tarling, of Lily Cottage, Steeple Bumpstead was reported POW and RAF Sgt Les Lewis, Blackmore End, returned after serving for a spell with the French underground following his escape after being reported MIA, as was L/Cpl Aubrey Barnes, Park Cottages Gosfield. However Capt George Nott, a Halstead solicitor of Wickham St Paul Hall was KIA.

On a more cheerful note wounded American soldiers and airmen were entertained at Hoses Farm, Toppesfield by Mrs Leslie Plummer, and it was the officers' turn at Spains Hall, Finchingfield, many of them cycling to the village.

Despite the war the villages' flower and vegetable shows went on proving the spirit of the local people could not be dimmed. A few games of cricket and bowls were played.

The number of evacuees continued to grow and the UDC were obliged to take over property for billets, at Vic-

Halstead Auxiliary Fire Service. Back row left to right: Archie King, Sonny Clift, Cyril Wiseman, Aubrey Porter, Eddie Jarman, Peter Francis, Bob Norman and Harry Butcher.

Second row: Fred Thompson, Albert Williams, Ted Webber, Fred King, Tom Fowler, George Lock, Bob Cooper, Ron Tyrell, Reuben Wiffen, Alan Arnold, Bill Harvey, George Abbot and Charlie Wright.

Third row: Claude Reeve, Mun Harvey, Herb Hostler, Captain W. A. Nicholson, Albie Diss, Ted Butcher, Joe Jackson and Dick Kibble.

Front row: Fred Bocking, Les Gould, Reg Kibble, Jack Osborne, Harry Goldsmith, Stan Rippingale, Bert Staines and Jack Hulme.

The Market Hill was not so busy in the wartime years when traffic used to pass either side of the fountain.

Halstead Civil Defence section. Back row left to right Bernard Briars and Billy Cook. Front: Jim Bartholomew, Lil Scillitoe, Ernie Pettit and Jimmy Suckling.

A B26 Marauder of the 323rd Bomb Group of the US Ninth Air force based at Earls Colne with the bomb doors open for a raid over enemy occupied Europe.

Based at Gosfield were A20 Havocs of the 410th Bomb Group of the USAAF. Above is 'Helen' which was painted in matt black for night duties.

Signals section of Halstead Home Guard. Back row, left to right: George Boreham, Alf Fairbanks, ? McGregor, Jack Gard, Alfie Crone, Frank Drury, Harold Stribling, John Sayward and Tom Fowler. Front: Barbara Sparkes (Root), Ethel Davey (Lock), Lt G. R. Croxall, Lenna Rayner and Peggy Britton (Chinnery).

Halstead Co-operative Society played its part in War Weapons Week by giving the splendid sum of £5,000.

This B17 Flying Fortress crashed at Bailey Hill farm, Birdbrook, and burnt out killing all ten crew. It came from the 381st Bomb Group at Ridgewell.

US Flying Fortress from Ridgewell crashed and burnt out at Lorkins Farm, Twinstead on 5 May 1944.

A Flying Fortress of the 381st Bomb Group standing superbly in the Ridgewell sunshine on 1 July 1944.

Castle Hedingham Home Guard. Standing left to right: Vic Sandford, Arthur Ward (Tater), Alf Wheeler, Walter Corder, Les Ambrose, Ernie Boreham, ? Collar, Bill Walford, Sid Williams, Arthur Maxim, Herbert Lorkin, Arthur Earey, ? Downs, ? Harrington, Michael Brown, ?? and Tom Jones. Seated, left to right: Cuthbert Mitson, Percy Stock, Cyril Philp and Fred Ellis.

All ten crew were killed when this Ridgewell B17 Flying Fortress crashed on take off, into Blooms Wood, Wethersfield Road, Sible Hedingham.

An American serviceman from Ridgewell airfield who made a bet that VE-Day would occur before 1 July 1945 pays off his debt, watched by a crowd of residents outside the Waggon & Horses, Great Yeldham, on 17 May, 1945.

Halstead Ambulance Service line up at Nether Priors, the HQ of the ARP. Back row left to right: Winston Smith, Jimmy Gurteen and Bert Hunt. Centre: Joyce Pole, Peggy Cooper, Molly Darling, Charlie Smith, Margaret Weston, Doris Pole and Hettie Barker. Front: Olive Joyce, Phyllis Turp, Phyllis Grunwell, George Coe, Albert Bright (CO), Mary Waters, Edna Barker and Phyllis Sargent.

Bulmer Home Guard

Left to right
Back row: Dennis Cardy, Jack Cornell, Phillip Wells, James Raymond, Arthur Butcher, Ernest Smith, Thomas Rowe, Sidney Rowe, Eric Messent and Edmund Raymond.
Middle row: Lawrence Coe, Ralph Coe, Bernard Rowe, Albert Raymond, Leonard Raymond, Harry (Nicki) Cansell, Walter Tomson, Phillip Rowe, Walter Wright, William Rowe, Frank Surridge and Derek Felton.
Front row: Robert Smith, John Cardy, Thomas Radley, Fred Felton, Charles Raymond, Lt. Joe Hitchcock, Robert Sporn, Harry Cansell, Ernest Lott and Walter Earl.

On parade are men of the 1st Platoon, D company, 15th Battn, Essex Home Guard at Sible Hedingham, outside their school HQ. Back row left to right: J. Moules, H. Everitt and S. Earey. Centre: E. Finch,——,——,——, and E. Letch. Front: Lt Norman Vagg and Capt. P. W. Putnam.

In the late summer of 1944 the flying bomb, or Doodlebug as it was better known began to be seen in the skies over East Anglia. By the end of the war some had fallen within the Halstead district.

In early 1945 a British fighter shot down a V1 Flying Bomb, which crashed and severely damaged No 40 Tilbury Road, Tilbury Juxta Clare. The original gate post still stands!

In May 1944 the headquarters of the No. 1163 Colne Valley Air Training Corps was opened in Mallows Field by Air-Marshall Sir Leslie Gossage. Third left was the CO, Sir Ronald Long.

Halstead Red Cross. Back row left to right: Doris Sewell, Evelyn Doe, Chrissie Jay and Doris Whitfield.
Centre row: Doris Bowyer, Mrs. Butler, Flo Reeve, Gladys Pole, E. Wiseman, E. May and E. Stedman.
Front row: Maggie Chamberlain, Mary Nash, Mrs. Nash, Connie Munson (CO), Mrs. King, E. Barnes and Doris Norman.

On 13 July 1944 this B17 Flying Fortress from Ridgewell crashed into the railway cutting near Weybridge Farm, Great Yeldham, killing eight crewmen. The Colne Valley was without its railway for a few days.

Two stalwarts of Halstead's 'Dig for Victory' Campaign, Arthur Fitz and Sidney Pole who was a town councillor.

Halstead Civil Defence team had been specially trained in the use of a Bren gun in case of emergencies. Left to right: Joe Root, Ron Parr, Alec Cocksedge, Bill Fitz and Albert Martin.

After the war the Ashford Lodge P.O.W. camp at Halstead was used as accommodation for young families without a home including (above left) Albert Cross a founder member of the Halstead and District Local History Society and (above right) the present Mrs. June Needham.

The Public Gardens, Halstead in the spring of 1944, with US servicemen taking a well earned rest as they chat with local girls.

This Heinkel III crashed on Mr C.V. Wordley's land at Peverells Farm, Colne Engaine on 30 August, 1940.
Many sightseers came to look at the aircraft during the time it was waiting for removal and over £100 was collected from them for the local Fighter Fund.

Edward G. Robinson, famous American film star christens B17 Flying Fortress of the 381st Bomb Group at Ridgewell on 5 July 1944.

Marks Hall, the red brick Elizabethan manor house which stood on the edge of Earls Colne airfield and sadly demolished in the early 1960's was the headquarters of the United States Ninth Air Force.

More than 4000 men and their guests packed a hangar at Ridgewell to hear international singing star Bing Crosby in September 1944.

International newspaper magnate William Randolph Hearst, Jr, was a reporter with the INS when he visited the 323rd Bomb Group at Earls Colne. He is second from right after having flown a mission in a B26 Marauder.

k Steward, Fred Ward, Ralph Vince, George Sly, Jack Hardy, Marshall Wicks,
Rayner, Leo Pendle, Bertie Owers, Ernie Dean, George Curtis, Harry Goldsmith,
Anderson, Captain Taylor (CO), Harold Bragg, John Frost, Jack Rippingale,
Bert Hawkes, Ernie Sayward, Ted Hardy, Bill Sturmer, Sam Pye, Doug Fleet,
mberson, Ernie Slyfield, Tom Mayes, ? Pretty and George Miles.

A company, 15th Battalion Essex Home Guard at Nether Priors, Halstead just before stand down in December 1944.

Back row left to right: Les Cook, George Bragg, Reg Bullard, Albert Bowyer, Ken Tofts, Jack Deal, Fred Root, — — and Horace Slyfield.

Second row: — —, — —, Len Spurgeon, Les Sibley, Percy Root, ? Williamson, — —, ? Ward, Billy Williams, ? Ewens, George Tibble, — —, Harry Wicker, ? Plumb, — —, Ernie Hayward, Walter Davies, Reg Tansley, Bill Kemp, Jack Root, Bill Rose, Charlie Kemp, Frank Wilkin and ? Lee.

Centre: Alf Bearham, George Brazier, ? Boreham, David Scillitoe, Reg Williamson, Ernie Smoothy, ? Hutley, Herbie Cable, George Drury, ? Keeble, Bill Bowles, Alex Payne, — —, Ralph Bird, Jack Bacon, Jack Tofts, John Marsh, Alex Smith, Ben Hart, Len Finch, Arthur Johnson and Harry Parker.

Fourth row: Alf Mortimer, — —, ? Rulton, ? Cracknell, — —, Arthur Bridge, Frank Mower, Bill Waters, Rueben Bowles, Harry Wellington, Alf Corder, Basil Osborne, Albert Chaplin, Vic Wilkin, Stanley Bush, George Rayner, Gerald Arnold, George Taylor, Bill Simpson, Jack Cutting, Charlie Ready, Harry Blackwell, Archie Diss, ? Taylor, Ashley Spurgeon, — — and Leo Lindekam.

Front row:
Sid Pudne
Sid Simm
Harold W

Believed to be the last Stirling to take off from Ridgewell, this aircraft belonged to No. 90 Squadron RAF, was under repair when its unit moved out, and the American 381st Bomb Group moved in May 1943, before it was repaired and flown out.

In early December 1944, Halstead's Home Guard Battalion was officially disbanded with due pomp and ceremony with a parade down the High Street, the salute being taken by Lt Col D. B. Rose outside the Eastern National Bus Company Depot.

Air Raid Wardens of Trinity parish, Halstead, line up in the Public Gardens after a parade, their HQ being the old police barracks, Trinity St, opposite the turning to Gosfield.
    Back row left to right: Ron Parr, Bill Fitz, Alan Dowsett, A. Foster, Albert Smith, Fred Smith and Albert Martin.
    Centre: Charlie Williams, Arthur Rogers, Cliff Sidy, Joe Root, Harold Townrow, Harold Benning, Sylvanus Binks, W.E. Patterson and Harry Butcher.
    Front: Percy Andrews, Stella Carter, Alec Cocksedge, Will Coote, Arthur Buck, Marion Owers, Jack Ablett, Miss Patterson and David Carter.

Another page in Halstead's war years was turned when the official disbandment of the Civil Defence Services took place at Nether Priors. This combined both urban and rural and was carried out by Mr. F. R. Foster, ARP Controller for Essex on Sunday 3 June, 1945.

All that was left of two Flying Fortresses that collided as they came into land at Ridgewell in early 1945. All twenty crewman were killed and the wreckage fell about half a mile from the base, in Belchamp St Paul.

Over 40 aircraft crashed in the area during the war and this RAF Stirling came down near St Margaret's Church, Tilbury-juxta-Clare on 16 November 1944 en route to Stradishall. The crew were unhurt.

A P47 Thunderbolt of the 365th Fighter Group based at Gosfield. The pilot Lt Col Robert L. Coffey, Jr, was shot down on 11 July 1944.

Great and Little Yeldham Platoons of the Home Guard in about 1944.

Back row:
Jack Laver, William Rulten, Bertie S. Rulton, Horace S. Allen, Leonard W. Cole, Charles W. Smith.
Second row:
George Henderson, Bruce Christison, George White, Charles Overall, Stanley Barber, Charles Backhouse, Fredrick Jobson, George H. Cansell, George E. Raymond, Benjamin Cranfield, George Louth?, Percival W. Yeldham, Fredrick Fuller, George Brown, Fredrick Tarbin, Cyril Ellis, Jack Overall, William Tarbin.
Third row:
Silas Smee, Fred Laver, ____?____, Edward Alliston, William Mizon, Frederick W. Deal, Thomas Towzer, Sidney Swallow, James Wright, Fredrick Martin, John H. Rulten, Bert Bevan, William H. Wilkin, Ernest Howe.
Fourth row:
Reginald Collar, Peter Callagher, William C. Turner, Christopher Lawrence, Hugh Cocks, Charles Deal, Stanley A. Tarbin, Derek Johnson, Edward Martin, Fredrick Rawlings, Victor Twitchett, George A. Argent, Sidney Angel, Thomas Smee, Frederick Allen, Bert Everitt.
Bottom row:
Jack Charlton, Alfred Turner, Edward Wass, Reginald Ince, Lieut. T.B. Meek, Lieut. Pentley, Lieut. Edward Filmer, Lt. Col. D.B. Rose, Capt. Baxter, Lieut. T.J. Archer, Thomas Lowery, Sgt. Robert Campbell, Jess Antrobus, Cpl. Cole, Cpl. Harold Rulten, Wilfred Taylor.

Halstead ARP. Back row left to right: Rita Warren, Connie Munson, Eileen Root, Bill Lorkin, Gladys Pole, Mary Nash, Joan Jeggo, Phyllis Turp and Bessie Warner.

Centre row: Dora Earey, Grace Martin, E. Wiseman, Chrissie Jay, Dot Ruggles, Mrs Nash, Mrs Coe, Edna Harrington, Alice Hart and Doris Whitfield.

Front row: Doris Norman, Peggy Kibble, Doris Bowyer, Dr D.T. Gemmell, Doreen Finch, Dr Ranson, Mrs Butler and Dorothy Smith.

Ginger's Brass Band celebrate peace at The George, Earls Colne. Back row left to right: John Sumner, Major Phillips, Percy Warren, Billy Poulter, Peter Willingham and Bob Matthews.
Centre row: Ginger Sumner, Mrs Dawson, George Boar, Jack Whittle, Reg Bragg, Doddie Wass and Dave Dawson (landlord).
Front row: Bill Reedar, Billy Poulter (Snr), Jim Pratt and Mrs Scillitoe.

The announcement of peace was received at Halstead Market Hill with the well known Radio Centre van in the midst of the proceedings.

toria Cottage, Colchester Road, and Jesmond, Kings Road, and a request was made for the British Restaurant to open on Sundays as was the case in Haverhill. The July figures showed an average of 175 main meals daily. A complaint was received that the shelters at Baylis' shop at 14 High St. Halstead was found closed five minutes after 'All Clear' and showed no signs of having been open and the steps were dirty. The surveyor was instructed to get them cleaned and see that the 'S' sign was fixed to the shelters for all to see. The General Purpose Committee reported during July the collections resulted in: waste paper — three tons; textiles — six cwt; bones — eight cwt, value £27/11/10d.

Killed in action were L/Cpl Les Stebbing, of Great Yeldham and Rfm Wally May, of Manfield, Halstead; RAF Sgt Dennis Tarbin, of Meads Farm, Toppesfield, and Capt A.E. Unwin, of Baythorne Hall were WIA, and at RAF Basrah, LAC Edgar Britton, of Stanley Road, Halstead was in his billet next to an empty bed when an old school chum, AC Gordon Bradford of Hedingham walked in to fill the vacancy!!

Holidays at Home Week was a great success in the town, and included horticultural shows, beauty contests, baby and rabbit shows, childrens sports, decorated bicycles and a ladies ankle competition. A Fun Fair and carnival was held at the Waterworks Meadow in Parsonage Street which proved to be very popular, the entire festivities raising £581.

In August a piscatorial tragedy took place at Gosfield Lake. It was found the water had been contaminated when it was discovered many fish were floating on the surface on Monday morning, and by the evening the numbers had increased considerably. By Tuesday morning it was a tragic scene with hundreds of fish gasping at the water's edge and it was easy to pick up tench 3/4 lbs, several golden carp of 30" long, scores of 15 lb pike and there were eels attempting to leave the water. It took at least six cart loads to dispose of the dead fish at the end of the week.

At Twinstead four young brothers were killed when they attempted to take a bomb fuse to pieces: Eric 18, Dennis 16, Gordon 12 and Norman 10, the sons of Reuben Harrington of The Green.

LAC Fred Dixey of Hampers Farm, Little Maplestead, who served in the RAF, was on leave in Rome when he entered St Peters Cathedral, and while there was spoken to by the Pope. L/Cpl Chris Portway of Monks, Great Maplestead was reported POW.

During the autumn the infamous Flying Bomb, commonly called 'Doodlebug' began to make its appearance over the skies of Essex. For several weeks along with Ray Norman, Royston Bullard and the late Jimmy Cook, I used to watch these Doodlebugs being attacked by RAF fighters as we sat on a grassy bank that used to run along part of West Road.

In October a genuine Doodlebug was on display at the Head Street fire station as well as an exhibition of photographs. I could not be certain if it was the same one, but I definitely can remember a Doodlebug on a low loader on display at the little car park of the Eastern National garage. I was among a few lads who sat astride it like a horse when a photographer took some shots. (I've never seen them since, but would love to know what happened to the pictures)

At the UDC Meeting members heard that Essex Education Committee had definitely decided to go ahead with the purchase of land at Bois Hall Farm for the erection of a senior school (now Ramsey), but Bert Owers spoke against it being built 'In the wilds of Coggeshall Pieces' as the fields were known. Despite repeated efforts for a second siren the County Council refused the UDC request, however Samuel Courtauld Limited offered to make their hooter available in the event of an emergency.

Reported MIA were L/Cpl John Beaney, Station Road, Albert Taylor, Bridge Street, both Earls Colne. Pte Maurice Kemp of Blue Bridge, Halstead was KIA. Two more brothers met abroad: RAF LAC Stan Tyler of New Street, Halstead met Rfn Bill in Italy, while Cfmn Bill Amos of Belchamp St Paul, serving in REME met his uncle, Dvr Stan Clements, RASC, also of Belchamp.

A Queen's Messenger convoy visited Halstead, which consisted of about a dozen vehicles and was capable of feeding 6,000 people. It aroused great interest in the town, and included a mobile field kitchen with 24 boilers, a 300 gallon water van, several food store vans, four canteens and a welfare vehicle. The visit in the bus park was sponsored by the HUDC and the personnel were entertained to tea at the British Restaurant.

Steps were being taken to consider a restricted form of street lighting either by gas or electricity, it was announced at the meeting of the HUDC, which met on Saturday afternoon!

Canon Thomas H. Curling, died aged 72, after 32 years as vicar of St Andrews,Halstead. He was a keen archaeologist and took an interest in all local affairs.

Halstead Home Guard stood down in December 1944. The parade was some 900 strong and assembled at Courtaulds Sports Ground in Colchester Road, the CO Lt Col D.B. Rose reading a message from HM King in a special Army Order of the Day. "The Home Guard has reached the end of its long tour of duty under arms, but I know that your devotion to duty, to our land, your comradeship, your power to work your hardest at the end of the longest day will discover new outlets for patriotic service in time of peace. History will say that your share in the greatest of all our struggles for freedom was a vitally important one. You have given your service without thought of reward. You have earned in full measure your country's gratitude."

Apparently as the war was going the Allies' way it seemed the Home Guard was becoming unnecessary.

HUDC had a problem at their meeting deciding what to do about the unwanted Great Yeldham fire engine. Originally it belonged to Halstead, but the Merryweather machine had seen better days and the parish council considered it worth only £30 as scrap. It was thought possible it could go to a museum and until a decision was made it was stored in a barn at Lovington's Farm.

News of serving local men revealed: RAF cadet Peter Mitson was killed in training flight in Arizona, USA; also KIA were Douglas Whitfield (RN), of Balls Chase: Cyril Rowland, Box Mill, both Halstead and Pte Albert Higgleton, Coggeshall Road, Earls

Colne. Taken POW were Cpl John Beaney, Station Road, Earls Colne and Percy Creswell, Steeple Bumpstead, while Jack Crysell of Windmill Road, Halstead was WIA. The Finch brothers of Trinity Road, Halstead met in Germany, L/Bdr Dick and Sgt Len, both in the RA, but Lt George Goodchild of Great Yeldham Hall was KIA in south east Asia.

The Minister of Town and Country Planning announced in December that under the Greater London Plan several Essex towns are to be expanded, Margaretting, Ongar and Harlow. He noted that Halstead and Braintree have something of the busy, rather crowded London atmosphere about them, and that the latter along with Bocking should be capable of absorbing about 30,000 persons. How right he turned out to be.

Local companies Charles Portway and the Tortoise Foundry report their contributions to the war effort with many castings and machinery going abroad between September 1939 and September 1944. Over 8,000 tons of castings were produced, 85,000 stoves and 780 bakers ovens by a total of 136,700 man hours.

* * * * * * * * * * * * * * * * * *

Halstead even had its own Prisoner of War camp. It was at Sudbury Road and was part of Ashford Lodge, being situated in the field opposite Constantine Cottages, at the junction of the road to Colne Engaine and Star Stile cricket ground. The original bell mouth kerbed entrance can still be seen. It opened during the summer of 1944 and a former accounts captain, Maurice Wickens, now living in Churchill Avenue recalls that it was

originally built for the US Army and had about 50 huts. It was officially designed as HQ 129 Italian Labour Battalion, Ashford Lodge, Halstead.

Known locally as Golden Meadow Camp, it housed about 500 Italians, later some Germans, and was the HQ of several other POW camps in the vicinity. There were about 100 POWs at a camp at The Auberies, Bulmer, and a similar one in the village near the church housing about the same; Borley Green 100; Liston Hall 100; Boxford 100 and Stoke by Nayland 200.

Prisoners were paid 5/- per week (25p) to be spent in the camp shop and 4/- which could be spent at local shops or picture houses. In late 1944 Italy had already surrendered and the POWs in the main were a very peaceful bunch. They were employed on agricultural work on local farms, and were a common sight in their green battledress of the co-operative personnel, whilst those non-co-operatives (those who hated the British or later on, the Germans) had a chocolate coloured uniform with yellow diamonds sewn on.

Maurice Wickens recalls it was a Mr Russell who was the camp labour officer and responsible for allocating the required number of workers to each farm; also the camp commandant a Lt Col W.G. Petherick, who is still alive in Cornwall, close to 80 years old.

He also remembers the three ton truck which used to collect the beer from Fremlins Brewery in Trinity Street (now the Council Yard) where Percy Brown was foreman, and also had to travel to Bury St Edmunds for razor blades and cake from the NAAFI depot. He never did know why these items could not be delivered with the normal rations!

There was a Roman Catholic Church in one hut as well as the usual messes and a hospital of sorts, even a Papal Nuncio attended the camp on one occasion to give spiritual comfort to his countrymen.

Maurice became friendly with several POWs and until recently received Christmas cards from them. When he left in September 1945 there were mostly Germans in the camp for nearly all the Italians had been repatriated.

However when the dust finally settled in Europe not all the German POWs went home. For some there was nothing to go home to. Many had lost contact with their families and their houses had long since been destroyed. So some stayed behind, married local girls brought up families and became integrated with local society.

One, Kurt Gottschalk, even came back after going home. He liked the Colne Valley and its people so much while he was here, and he vowed to return and settled in Great Yeldham.

He recalls that he was often on farm work and that he took the opportunity to snare rabbits which he used to sell to the British Restaurant for 2/6d (12½p).

There was little money for the POWs so they used to dig a local garden for a packet of cigarettes or a bottle of beer. During a walk one day he came across a consignment of broken chocolate bars in a barn which were destined for pig food. But he smelled business and it was not long before the chocolate was being melted down in the huts and poured into homemade moulds and wrapped in silver paper which was 'acquired', to sell to local children who very seldom saw chocolate, let alone eat it.

The manufacture of slippers also became a highly successful venture, these being made of cardboard and rope made from re-cycled sacks, and sales of these at the British Restaurant saw a very remunerative operation under way. However a nationally known shoe manufacturer got wind of the scheme and waved the 'big stick' and that was the end of that!

Like men of all races the Germans liked a drink and as they could not buy any, and being forbidden to enter pubs, they decided to make their own. The still was made from a variety of pipes and other materials they could scrounge, and there were plenty of vegetables and fruit as ingredients.

When all the POWs had left the camp, the local authority attempted to make the huts uninhabitable to prevent squatters, but the Englishman, being what he was, failed to be deterred, and many who returned from the wars to set up home with a new wife, soon brought back the huts into use as a home. Often a midnight stroll would produce a door or window from somewhere and it was not long before the camp came back to life again.

Of course the local authority soon spotted more revenue and the squatters were allowed to stay, and it was not until the housing estates in Halstead and district began to spring up that the huts began to empty and only the entrance now shows that anything was ever there.

1945

On the salvage front the army's Eastern Command announced that in the last six months (0f 1944) 187,992 gallons of waste oil had been received which saw a 15% reduction in refining; waste paper totalled 4,561 tons and scrap metal 16,775 tons.

Meantime Bomber Command announced the RAF were hammering Germany almost every night and the Americans doing so by day, which included the B17s from Ridgewell with the Flying Fortresses of the 381st Bomb Group. Although it was in the depths of winter technology made it possible to bomb through clouds. It was called — Radar.

Reports of serving men showed Gnr Charlie Beckwith of Mount Pleasant was POW in Far East as was Pte Arthur Cox, of Bumpstead Hall Cottages, Helions Bumpstead. Gosfield man, RAF Sgt Mortyn Downing was presented with a Polish award as a token of thanks for his efforts on a secret trip to Moscow flying an Avro York.

At Sible Hedingham the local branch of the WEA held a series of lectures on 'Children of the USSR'.

Over five years earlier, Halstead Congregational Church had opened a forces canteen in their hall which had proved most successful with £13,000 having passed over the counter and £455 being given away to Army welfare funds.

Halstead Food Committee refused to grant a licence to sell fruit to the proprietors of The Florists, in the High Street, for it was thought there were plenty of greengrocers in the town to satisfy demand!

Sgt John Lock of New Street Halstead was granted his RAF wings, while two former 1163 ATC men followed suit — Joe Miller, Kings and Terry Warren of Tidings Hill, both of Halstead; F/Sgt Bill Collar, Kirby Hall Road, Castle Hedingham, was awarded the DFM.

The C Company, Army Cadets, of the 11th Bttn Essex Regiment was started in Halstead with their HQ at the Drill Hall, in Pretoria Road, and after only a few weeks was 82 strong including six officers.

The UDC decided to stop street lighting in Halstead as piloted planes had been seen over southern England (presumably they meant the enemy!) and emphasised the necessity of maintaining the blackout regulations. Looking further ahead to the end of the war chairman Sid Pole suggested starting a Welcome Home fund, which met with unanimous agreement.

In March the UDC agreed to the siting of 20 temporary dwellings on the Coggeshall Pieces, providing they did not interfere with new school (later to become the Ramsey School). However these 'prefabs' as they were known, eventually finished up at the top of Windmill Road, Halstead and were still in use over 20 years after the war.

As the war was drawing to a close it was obvious that the people were beginning to lead a normal life again with many institutions calling meetings and activities being arranged.

Former POW Cpl Bill Smith, of Lit-

57

tle Yeldham returned home after nearly three years of internment.

A public meeting was called at the council chambers in Red House to discuss 'Holidays at Home' later in the year and the UDC agreed that when the peace announcement was received all church bells would be rung and that Adams Brewery would fire their cannon. The Braintree Town Band would play on the Market Hill (though what the town of Braintree would do without their own band at the peace announcement was not certain!!!), as well as agreeing to resume street lighting, albeit on the casting vote of the chairman, Jack Root.

Mr R.A. Butler spoke at a meeting at Pebmarsh on the tragic death of President Roosevelt, saying "We have lost a great friend who came to help us at our darkest hour, giving us the tools to do the job" as had been requested by Winston Churchill.

During April Dvr Cecil Kemp, of Belchamp Road, Tilbury-juxta-Clare was KIA with the BIA, but seven POWs were liberated: Pte John Eldred, Mallows Field; Pte Reg Cook, Colne Road, both Halstead; Pte John Beaney, Station Road and Tpr Stan Frost, Lion Cottage, both Earls Colne; Pte Don Cutmore, Hyde Green, Blackmore End; F/Sgt Lewis Rollingson, High Street Green, Sible Hedingham and Pte Wilf Clark, White Colne.

Former Halstead Town FC skipper Mick Osborne, of Trinity Road, Halstead serving in the RAF in Cyprus, played for an England XI who beat a Scotland XI.

Late in April news filtered through that Pte Ron Bartholomew, of Colchester Road, White Colne and Gnr Ron Wiffen, of Ridgewell were KIA in Italy.

At the beginning of May more local servicemen who had been POWs were released: Pte John Bullard, West Road (who had worked in a salt mine); Sgt Albie Smith, Factory Terrace and Gnr Cliff Sudbury, Stanley Road, all Halstead; Gnr Wilf Higgleton, Colchester Road, Chappel; Gnr Albert Reeve, Gestingthorpe and Pte Edgar Wiseman, Little Maplestead.

Peace finally came to Europe on Monday, 7 May, but it was the following day when Prime Minister Winston Churchill made the official proclamation saying "Yesterday morning at 02.41 hrs, at General Eisenhower's HQ, General Jodl, representative of the German High Command and Grand Admiral Doenitz, the designated head of the German State — the Act of General Surrender of all German land, sea and air forces in Europe to the Allied Expeditionary Force, and simultaneously to the Russian High Command."

"The German war is therefore at an end. The injury she inflicted on Poland, then others, Great Britain and the United States of America call for justice and retribution. We must now devote all our strength and resources to the completion of our task both at home and abroad. Long live the cause of freedom. Long live the King."

A huge banner bearing 'God save the King' was hung across Halstead High Street, and every shop was strewn with flags and bunting. Church bells rang throughout the Colne Valley and there was a huge crowd on the Market Hill to hear the Prime Minister's announcement, which was followed by the clerk of the UDC Ronald Long reading the resolution of the council 'On the occasion of VE-Day, 8 May, 1945, the council place on record their sympathy with all who suffered hardship, loss or bereavement in any way and express their sincere wish for a speedy return to all the men and women of Halstead who are serving their country at home or overseas. They also thank the people of Halstead who served in the Civil Defence Services to guard the town and acknowledge the splendid spirit shown in their devotion to duty, loyalty, and steadfastness through the difficult years which have brought us victory!

The crowd then made their way to the Public Gardens for more rejoicing where a service of thanksgiving was held with all the ministers of the town taking their place in the bandstand. During the evening the Braintree Town Band (who else!!) played selections and there was dancing on the centre lawn. Inevitably all the pubs were granted extensions but only until 11.30pm, which the magistrate, Frank Vaizey, thought was enough, despite Inspector Billett pointing out it was midnight in other towns!

The following day the celebrations continued with childrens sports, dog shows, rabbit shows, decorated prams, but the rain did not damp spirits in the evening when a concert took place under the direction of Will Coote, who took part with Alf Wicker, Bob Ross and T.J. Rattee (former station master) and called the Halstead Male Voice Quartet. Community singing followed with Alfred Farmer as accompanist (He was the late headmaster of Holy Trinity School).

Every town and village throughout the land all staged their own celebrations which included church services, but despite the end of hostilities people were warned to be on guard about shortages of most things, for rationing was still the order of the day.

Other local men who returned were: Dennis Lee, Windmill Road; Harold Lock, Kings Road; both Halstead; Rodney Hatfield, Castle Hedingham; Christopher Portway, Great Maplestead; Russell Carter, Sible Hedingham; Arthur Simmons, Little Maplestead, while Dick Finch of Trinity Road, Halstead was presented with a certificate for outstanding service by Field Marshal Montgomery.

The Civil Defence was officially disbanded at Nether Priors in June.

There had been 1,052 alerts; high explosive bombs dropped 58 in the UDC area and 67 in RDC; four unexploded bombs, UDC and 67 RDC; parachute mines 2 and 11. Approximately 4,900 incendiaries in the whole area; oil bombs 17; phosphorous 15; anti-personnel 46; flying bombs 11; long range rockets (V2s) 1; crashed aircraft including three enemy 43; 2 barrage balloons; 36 casualities and 1 fatality.

Property damage included 2,050 homes and shops; 27 office and business premises; 6 industrial premises, 11 churches, 5 schools and 2 cinemas.

Come August, the Japanese surrendered and there was peace in the world once more.

Home Guard Stand Down.

3rd DECEMBER, 1944.

The 15th Essex Batt. Home Guard

will be holding their

STAND DOWN PARADE

on the FACTORY SPORTS GROUND, Colchester Road,
Halstead, on **3rd December, 1944.**

The Parade will be Addressed by

The Commanding Officer & The Rt. Hon. R. A. Butler, M.P.

The Battalion will March through the Town at
12.15 p.m. led by the

BAND of the GLOUCESTERSHIRE REGIMENT

THE SALUTING BASE

will be established at the Eastern National Garage, High Street.

THE SALUTE will be taken by

Air Vice Marshall J. R. SCARLETT-STREATFEILD, C.B.E.

accompanied by Brigadier R. W. McLEOD.

'A' Coy. 15th Essex Batt. Home Guard

GRAND FINAL DINNER
and SOCIAL EVENING

SATURDAY, December 2nd, 7.30 p.m.
At The Drill Hall, Halstead.

ENTERTAINMENT by the "HALSTEAD REVELLERS"

TICKETS **1/6.** including all Refreshments

From any member of the Social Committee, and must be obtained on or
before WEDNESDAY, NOVEMBER 29th.

Dress—CleanFatigue.

APPENDIX 1
INCIDENT FILE

A list of bombings and similar incidents in the Halstead area.

1940

25/6   Steeple Bumpstead — H Ex bomb at Chapel St; four buildings damaged.

28/6   Ashen — four small bombs.

15/8   Ridgewell — two bombs in field.

16/8   Halstead — H Ex bombs dropped but no casualties (no location given).

16/8   Colne Engaine — H Ex bombs in Elms Hall Rd, one soldier killed and two injured.

16/8   Gosfield — H Ex bombs, no casualties.

17/8   Halstead — UXB near Balls Farm House.

21/8   Stambourne — H Ex bombs.

21/8   Belchamps — one small bomb.

25/8   Halstead — two H EX (one UXB) in paddock at Blue Bridge House.

25/8   Gosfield — small bomb at Hawkswood Farm, set three stacks on fire.

26/8   Halstead — enemy aircraft down at Burtons Green.

27/8   Helions Bumpstead — one bomb and UXB in Pole Green meadows.

27/8   Gosfield — one UXB at Aylwards Farm, near lake.

29/8   Stambourne — three UXB near Rectory; two H Ex at Sadlers Field and four small bombs at Tagley Farm.

31/8   Colne Engaine — German aircraft down at Peverall's Farm but only slightly damaged. One crew member dead, three injured and one unhurt.

7/9   Gosfield — small bomb on stack at Home Farm, Gosfield Hall.

11/9   Belchamp Walter — small bomb.

11/9   Gosfield — Small bomb.

11/9   Bulmer — small bomb.

11/9   White Colne — H Ex bombs.

11/9   Bures Hamlet — H Ex bombs.

11/9   Lamarsh — H Ex bombs, but no damage or casualties.

18/9   Gosfield — small bomb at Hawkswood Farm.

18/9   Greenstead Green — small bomb at Perce's Farm.

18/9   Sible Hedingham — small bomb at Runalong Farm (all under control!)

19/9   Gosfield — two bombs in spinney near Gosfield Place Lodge, and 12 more at Aylwards Farm.

19/9   Sturmer — three H Ex bombs.

19/9   Colne Engaine — two H Ex near Brickhouse Farm.

21/9   Halstead area — two unidentified planes dropped a large bale of cotton wool which came down in fine particles. Specimen sent to Professor Bedson at Billericay.

22/9   Sible Hedingham — one H Ex near Blackmore End and a land mine at Cut Maple causing damage to houses.

61

22/9 Stambourne — tracer bullets burnt out three stacks at Lower Green Farm.

23/9 New England — Colne Valley Arms, Bumpstead/Haverhill Rd junction blocked by UXB. Military on spot.

25/9 Birdbrook — Land mine exploded near Moat Farm, Finkle Green and blocked road causing slight damage.

26/9 Liston — small bomb caused slight damage to Rectory.

26/9 Belchamp St Paul — H Ex bomb possibly land mine exploded, but only slight damage.

4/10 Gt Yeldham — two H Ex bombs broke windows at Spencers.

4/10 Tilbury — one H Ex bomb broke window and door at Warren Cottage.

5/10 Helions Bumpstead — small bombs in beet and potato fields near Pole Green Rd.

5/10 Sible Hedingham — oil bomb down at Morris Green.

6/10 Wickham St Paul — three H EX and one oil bomb down in fields, but no casualties.

8/10 Earls Colne — one H Ex UXB 1¼ miles SW of village.

8/10 Foxearth — one oil bomb.

8/10 Birdbrook — one oil bomb, no damage.

13/10 Birdbrook — Balloon 20ft in diameter near Steeple Bumpstead Rd, was taken to Halstead police station (see main story).

14/10 Baythorne End — eleven H Ex bombs in field, ten craters plus one UXB, no casualties.

16/10 Colne Engiane — H Ex parachute bomb in field between Knights and Cangle Farms.

16/10 Stambourne — H Ex bomb and oil bomb near Robin Hood End.

20/10 Earls Colne — two H Ex bombs on Coggeshall Rd.

20/10 Sible Hedingham — H Ex bomb at junction of A604 and A1017, known as Braintree Corner, Fractured gas mains and PO cables.

29/10 Sible Hedingham — six H Ex bombs in field near station and Rippers Yard.

1/11 Belchamp St Paul — UXB found south of Downs Farm, also parachute bomb.

1/11 Ashen — two H Ex bombs.

1/11 Sturmer — two small bombs.

4/11 Gosfield — one H Ex bomb down at rear of Petersfield Farm, slight damage to farmhouse but no casualties.

5/11 Twinstead/Alphamstone — six H Ex bombs in rural area, no damage.

6/11 Bures Hamlet — four H Ex bombs blocked Colchester Rd. Three houses slightly damaged but no casualties.

6/11 Pentlow — one H Ex bomb in rural area, no damage.

8/10 Earls Colne — eight H Ex bombs on Sheppards Row (?), two casualities and house demolished.

10/11 Halstead — two H Ex bombs down in Oak Rd, no damage but one UXB.

11/11 Pebmarsh — 15 H Ex bombs on fields at Oak Farm near to Maplestead Cock Woods causing broken windows.

11/11 Foxearth — four H Ex bombs caused slight damage to two cottages.

11/11 Burtons Green — eight H Ex bombs, no damage.

11/11 Earls Colne — five H Ex bombs, no damage.

11/11 Foxearth — 17 H Ex bombs, slight damage to cottages.

15/11 Halstead — Parachute mine on Tidings Hill at 21.25 hrs. Three people taken to hospital, ten others injured and 30 more were evacuated. Six houses badly damaged as well as shops in the High St.

15/11 Halstead — Parachute mine in field at Ayletts Farm near to Froyz Hall Farm. It exploded in mid air but no damage.

1941

5/1 Bulmer — H Ex and oil bomb in rural area.

30/1 Toppesfield — H Ex bomb in rural area.

16/2 Castle Hedingham — H Ex bomb killed one and injured 11 more.

16/2 Ridgewell — H Ex bomb in rural area.

16/2 Stambourne — H Ex bomb in rural area.

17/2 Ridgewell — H Ex bomb in rural area.

25/2 High Garrett — UXB closed road.

25/2 Stambourne — anti personnel bombs in rural area.

27/2 Alphamstone — H Ex bomb in rural area.

27/2 Gosfield — Parachute bomb demolished house near Pear Tree Farm, three injured.

8/3 Birdbrook — H Ex bomb near Ash Mill.

8/3 Steeple Bumpstead — H Ex bomb on Garlands Farm.

14/3 Gt Henny — small bomb in field near Park Farm.

14/3 Greenstead Green — small bombs near Perce's Farm and Whiting House and another towards Burton Green.

14/3 Halstead — small bomb down at The Cangle.

8/4 Ridgewell — two H Ex bombs in fields towards Baythorne End.

8/4 Gt Henny — two H Ex bombs near Gt Henny Mill.

16/4 Lt Henny — ten H Ex bombs in field near Gentry's Cottage which was damaged.

21/4 Steeple Bumpstead — three H Ex bombs.

21/4 Stambourne — eight H Ex bombs in rural area.

4/5 Middleton — H Ex bomb in rural area.

6/5 Alphamstone — H Ex bomb near Kings Farm blocked road between Cripple Corner and The Windmill pub.

11/6 Stambourne — seven H Ex bombs in rural area.

18/6 Bures Hamlet — Flares fell from British aircraft.

19/6 Birdbrook — 19 small bombs in field.

1942

30/7   Earls Colne — UXB west of Hop Green Farm, Coggeshall Rd.

1943

15/6   Helions Bumpstead — one H Ex bomb down but no damage.
14/7   Helions Bumpstead — three H Ex bombs in field, no casualties with a crater found at Steeple Bumpstead.
16/7   Earls Colne — two H Ex bombs but no casualties or damage.
3/10   Belchamp St Paul — one H Ex bomb in ploughed field.
15/10 Halstead — one H Ex bomb at White Ash Green, and another in Hedingham Rd causing one serious casualty and two slight.
15/10 Colne Engaine — one H Ex bomb in open field.
31/10 White Colne — two H Ex bombs near Bures road.
10/12 Gosfield — four H Ex bombs at Shardlows Farm; four at Petersfield Farm; five at Park Hall Farm; one at Harmas Farm and 14 on the airfield killing seven and injuring 37, also UXB.
10/12 Sible Hedingham — eight H Ex bombs near Gosfield Rd (part of same raids as above).
21/12 White Colne — one H Ex bomb at Wakes Hall and another at Bart Hall.

1944

21/1   Sible Hedingham — one H Ex bomb at Hopkins Farm.
21/1   Gosfield — two H Ex bombs at Liston Hall Farm and two more at Harmas Farm.
29/1   Helions Bumpstead — small bomb at Helions Farm.
4/2   Bures Hamlet — bomb container in field near Ferriers Farm.
20/2   Twinstead — enemy plane overhead, one crewman bailed out.
15/3   Colne Engaine — one small bomb dropped.
22/3   Earls Colne — one H Ex bomb and UXB on USAAF base, slight damage to five houses in Coggeshall Rd.
19/4   Belchamp St Paul — five H Ex bombs fell in wood.
27/4   Sible Hedingham — bombs jettisoned from allied aircraft, one house damaged.
16/6   Bures Hamlet — unknown type bomb caused fire damage.
9/7   Gosfield — Flying bomb down at Aylwards Farm, causing slight damage. (Known as a Doodlebug, was first in immediate area).
18/7   Gt Maplestead — Flying bomb down near Mill Farm, slight damage to house.
18/9   Toppesfield — Flying bomb fell on USAAF property at Hawkes Hall. Slight damage but no casualties.
20/9   Earls Colne — Crashed aircraft, believed to be Lancaster, down at Holmwood Farm, crew killed one cottage damaged and six tenants evacuated. America Rd was closed.

24/9 Great Yeldham   Flying bomb down north of Spencers drive, two houses severely damaged but no casualties.

26/9 Sible Hedingham — Flying bomb down in field south west of Hostages Farm. Slight damage to 21 houses and school, one woman died of shock residing a mile from the incident.

29/9 Baythorne End — Flying bomb caused extensive damage to Baythorne Hall and cottage, also minor damage to 45 houses and Baythorne Park the historical house (sic). No casualties.

8/10 Greenstead Green — Flying bomb down in field causing slight damage to church and school (This possibly was a US P47 Thunderbolt from Boxted, a commemorative plaque to pilot in church).

23/10 Lamarsh — Flying bomb down in field damaging roof and windows of house near Edgars Farm and Lion Inn. Also minor damage to 14 other houses.

13/12 Sible Hedingham — Flying bomb down damaging Rookwoods House, the Senior School, Rippers and the Gas Office.

1945

6/2 Halstead — A US practice bomb damaged top of Mitchell Ave when down ten yards from nearest house.

6/2 Halstead — Long range rocket (V2) down 400 yards north of Blamsters Farm causing slight damage to 230 houses, 42 shops, three churches two factories, school , cinema and telephone wires.

13/2 Borley — A US practice bomb dropped at Paynes Farm, slightly damaging 280 properties. (How?)

25/3 Stambourne — Steel Container, containing hand trolley complete with red parachute down at Great Nortons Farm.

13/4 Ovington — seven US practice bombs exploded at Hall Farm.

APPENDIX II

AIRCRAFT CRASHES IN
HALSTEAD AREA

N.B. Aircraft crashes were not the responsibility of the Civil Defence to report before September 6th 1940.

* * * * * * * * * *

30.8.40 — A German aircraft HE III came down at Colne Engaine at 17.39 hrs. There was a crew of five, three injured, one dead and one unhurt in the wreck which was at Peveralls Farm.

14.10.41 — RAF Tiger Moth (W 51014) came down at 17.45 hrs on Earls Colne airfield, and which was based at RAF Hunsdon.

29.10.41 — RAF Wellington (K 1177) down at Birds Green Farm, Sible Hedingham at 03.15 hrs. The aircraft from No 75 Squadron at Feltwell was burnt out. Four crew were safe but two were missing.

12.4.42 — RAF Spitfire down at Catley Cross Corner, Wickham St Paul, at 11.00 hrs. It was out of control and crashlanded, the wreckage caught fire burning the body of the pilot which was not recovered. A portion of his head was found in a field nearby and picked up by an ambulance from RAF Stradishall.

13.5.42 — RAF fighter (?) N. DK 43, from RAF Watton came down near Bulmer brickfields, half a mile from the Hedingham-Sudbury Road at 13.50 hrs. The aircraft and pilot Sgt J. Hall (No. 1210980) were intact.

19.5.42 — RAF fighter came down and completely smashed at 16.15 hrs opposite Boarded Barn Farm, Helions Bumpstead. One crewman dead and another seriously injured. It was thought to be from Castle Camps.

17.6.42 — RAF Wellington down at Whittingham Meadows, Spains Hall Road, Finchingfield, behind the police houses at 04.55 hrs. The crew of six are safe but the co-pilot was injured. Aircraft from Mildenhall.

15.7.42 — RAF Hurricane down and burnt out at Birchwood, 50 yards from the Halstead-Bulmer road at 12.00 hrs. The pilot was killed.

15.7.42 — RAF Hurricane down intact at Ovington Hall Farm, 200 yards south of farmhouse at 13.00 hrs. Aircraft from Wittering marked SA-N, with pilot unhurt.

5.10.42 — RAF Wellington down at Boyton Hall Finchingfield, 500 yards east of Howe St. The aircraft was burnt out, two bodies were found, one named Howell. At 19.55 hrs.

6.10.42 — RAF Wellington down one mile east of Gestingthorpe church at 20.00 hrs and was burnt out. It came from Warboys (Hunts) with four crew safe and one missing.

24.11.42 — RAF Oxford (AT 778) down at Swan St, Sible Hedingham, 100 yards from rear of Monroe House at 18.15 hrs. Three men bailed out safely, but the aircraft, which came from Stradishall, was smashed up.

4.2.43 — RAF Tiger Moth (T 6909)

down at Greenstead Hall at 17.40 hrs but was intact. The pilot was uninjured and came from 22 EFTF at Cambridge.

12.5.43 — RAF fighter down at Monks Lodge, Gt Maplestead at 10.05 hrs. It was burnt out and the pilot dead.

9.8.43 — USAAF Marauder down near Florries Wood, Earls Colne — Gt Tey at 15.00 hrs, about 150 yards south east of Beackmans Farm. All six crew killed.

4.10.43 — RAF bomber down at White Gate Farm, Earls Colne, 400 yards south of the Bird in Hand pub. The crew bailed out safely but aircraft burnt out leaving UXB on board.

24.10.43 — USAAF Marauder from Station 162(?) down ¼ mile south of Wells Farm, Gosfield at 13.35 hrs. The aircraft No.42-31641 was smashed up, five crew injured and one killed.

4.1.44 — USAAF Fortress from Ridgewell (381st BG) down at Blooms Farm, Sible Hedingham, 120 yards north of Redbeards Wood at 07.50 hrs. All ten crew killed as the aircraft was fully loaded for a mission (42-31278).

14.2.44 — USAAF Havoc (A20) from Wethersfield (418th BG) down 400 yards north of Barnards Farm, Sible Hedingham at 09.00 hrs. The aircraft was smashed up completely, killing the pilot.

22.2.44 — An aircraft crashed at 22.11 hrs 200 yards east of Park Farm, Wickham St Paul. The burnt out aircraft is believed to be enemy, with one crewman injured and the rest died in the crash.

24.3.44 — USAAF Fortress (B17) from Ridgewell down at Bailey Hill Farm, Birdbrook at 05.50 hrs. All ten crew were killed on (43-8102) which also had two UXB.

31.3.44 — USAAF Fortress down at Wood Barn Farm, Belchamp St Paul at 15.30 hrs. (No other details given in records).

4.4.44 — USAAF Oxford trainer (R 5975) down at Hedingham Rd, Gosfield at 15.30 hrs. It did not catch fire and the occupants only slightly injured but no numbers were issued to the police.

17.4.44 — RAF Mosquito down at Boarded Barns Farm, Helions Bumpstead at 15.12 hrs. It came from Castle Camps and had only slight damage. The pilot F/O Bodet and crew were unhurt.

2.5.44 — USAAF Lightning (P38) from Wormingford (55th FG) at Purls Hill, Chelmshoe House, Gt Maplestead at 11.40 hrs. The pilot was killed.

5.5.44 — USAAF Fortress from Ridgewell down at Lorkins Farm, Twinstead at 10.57 hrs. It was 200 yards south of farmhouse, and four crew were safe. The aircraft No.42-97715.

6.5.44 — Thunderbolt (P47) down at Little Yeldham Hall, 400 yards north east of house at 10.25 hrs. Pilot dead, the aircraft being smashed and burnt out.

27.5.44 — A Mustang and Havoc collided at 18.50 hrs at Ashdon, crashing at Street Farm. Two Havoc crew killed immediately, but one crewman was saved by a woman, who went back for a fourth when it exploded killing both. It was thought the Havoc came from Wethersfield.

4.6.44 — USAAF Mustang down at Little Smiths Green, Steeple Bumpstead, at 20.00 hrs. It came from

Debden and the pilot was Lt Robert Kakerback.

17.6.44 — USAAF Havoc from Gosfield (410th BG) down at Seven Sisters Corner, Gestingthorpe, at 11.00 hrs. The aircraft was burnt out and the pilot, Wayne Brown was dead (No. 0412119).

13.7.44 — USAAF Fortress from Ridgewell down on railway line between Oaker Hill Bridge and Borleys Farm, Great Yeldham at 07.00 hrs. Aircraft was smashed up and burnt out. Two crew safe but rest killed.

15.7.44 — RAF Mosquito down at Herkestead Hall, Steeple Bumpstead at 18.55 hrs. Two crew dead and the aircraft believed from RAF Hunsdon.

23.7.44 — USAAF Marauder from Saling (Andrewsfield) down at Petersfield Farm, Gosfield. The B26 of the 322nd Bomb Group was not badly damaged, only propellers and undercarriage. Crew uninjured. Aircraft No. 431913.

4.8.44 — USAAF Fortress down at Rotten End, Wethersfield, at 10.00 hrs. The aircraft came from Ridgewell.

12.8.44 — USAAF Mustang from Debden down on Copy Farm, Helions Bumpstead at 19.30 hrs. The aircraft (No. 44-13372) was badly smashed but not burnt. The pilot bailed out and was only slightly injured.

13.8.44 — USAAF Havoc from Wethersfield (416th BG) down at Cuckoo Farm, Sible Hedingham at 20.50 hrs. Two crew dead and one seriously injured.

13.8.44 — USAAF Havoc from Wethersfield (416th BG) down at Cuckoo Farm, Sible Hedingham, 350 yards south west of the Wethersfield Rd at 22.25 hrs. The three crew members were all injured.

25.8.44 — USAAF Havoc from Gosfield (410th BG) down at Southey Green, Sible Hedingham at 20.50 hrs. Two crew dead and one seriously injured.

20.9.44 — RAF Lancaster down at Florries Farm, Great Tey/Holmwood Farm, Earls Colne at 16.00 hrs. All crew were killed and America Road was closed to traffic to Chalkney Wood. The aircraft was burnt out.

24.9.44 — A Flying Bomb (Doodlebug) V-1 came down at Tilbury Road, Great Yeldham, about 500 yards from Spencers Grange as the result of fighter action. Two houses were wrecked and requisitioned by the military, and 14 were damaged. Overhead cables and telephone lines were broken, but there were no casualties in this incident which occurred at 22.05 hrs.

1.10.44 — USAAF Thunderbolt down at Greenstead Green at 14.50 hrs as the result of a slight collision with a fighter. The pilot, Lt Dwight G. Belt, was killed. He was from the 56th FG from Boxted (Plaque in Greenstead Green church).

2.11.44 — USAAF Mustang down near Thatchers Arms, Mount Bures, at 1.415 hrs. The pilot was unhurt.

15.11.44 — RAF Stirling down 100 yards east of Tilbury church at 19.35 hrs. The aircraft (LK 432) was badly damaged and came from Stradishall, the two occupants slightly injured.

10.12.44 — USAAF Mustang down at Shardlows Farm, Gosfield at 04.45 hrs, 200 yards east of the farmhouse. The pilot had slight head injuries.

21.1.45 — Two USAAF Fortresses from Ridgewell came down at Tilbury, following a mid air collision at 20.45 hrs, 500 yards south of the Fox public house. Both aircraft were burnt out and all crewmen were killed.

3.2.45 — A bomber (B17 ?) came down at Tarbuns Farm, Coggeshall Road, Earls Colne at 00.15 hrs with UXBs on board. 23 people from seven cottages were evacuated. A later police report issued said four UXBs were defused by RAF, but one was still missing.

6.2.45 — A Mustang (USAAF ?) down at Collins Farm, Pebmarsh at 14.30 hrs. The pilot had bailed out and landed at Earls Colne airfield and was slightly hurt. The aircraft came from Duxford and was completely burnt out.

14.3.45 — USAAF Fortress (from Ridgewell?) down at 00.45 hrs half a mile east of Little Yeldham church. Of the crew of five, three were unhurt but two were taken to hospital.

APPENDIX III

Local airfields

An abbreviated history of the four
local airfields:-

Earls Colne

Of all the US air bases built in Britain
Earls Colne was one of the first and
came under the RAF in the early days,
Stradishall taking over from 26
August 1942. However it did not
become an operational airbase until
May 1943 when B17s of the 94th
Bomb Group moved in.

They stayed only a few weeks as the
runway was unsuitable for the heavy
bombers and they left for Rougham
near Bury St Edmunds in June. The
94th had one moment of importance
that led to changes in battle procedure
throughout the Eighth Air Force. On
returning from the last raid from
Earls Colne, the group were detailed
to land at Rougham, and as was the
custom in those early war years, the
gunners cleaned their guns out on the
way home over the North Sea. They
were immediately jumped by the Luft-
waffe, who sent nine bombers and
their ten-men crews down to oblivion
below and from that day, US gunners
were forbidden to clean their guns out
on the return journey.

In June the B26 Marauders of the
323rd Bomb Group moved in and
these medium bombers were in-
strumental in carpet bombing attacks
in support of the D-Day landings in
Normandy.

When they left in the autumn the
base stood quiet until the RAF moved

back in September 1944 when Nos 296
and 297 squadrons of 38 group arrived
flying Halifaxes IIIs after conversion
from Albemarles.

Several SOE operations followed
from December and Horsas joined
them in preparation for their part in
OPERATION VARSITY, the
crossing of the Rhine.

In the early spring of 1946 the
Halifaxes left and the station came
under the charge of a Care & Maintenance Unit, and eventually it rever-
ted to agriculture.

Gosfield

The Gosfield airfield was christened
with an air raid on the day it opened
— but only two bombs landed.

It was in October 1943 when the
365th Fighter Group of the Ninth Air
Force moved in with P47 Thun-
derbolts. After their initial training
proceded with tactical operations,
strafing and train busting, over France, before moving out in March 1944.

Then came the 410th Bomb Group,
whose A20 Havocs began their attacks
which led to the Normandy invasion
attacking gun installations, mar-
shalling yards and the rocket sites on
the French coast.

70

As the war went the Allies way the 410th moved to forward bases on the continent and the RAF arrived. After a brief stay the Martinets and Stirlings of the 1677 Target Towing Flight moved in and Gosfield became an important base in preparation for the assault to cross the Rhine. Here were Dakotas of Nos 271, 512 and 575 squadrons, which carried the paratroopers for one of the last big operations of the war in March 1945, and the airfield was closed completely later that year.

Ridgewell

The RAF were the first to arrive at Ridgewell when No 90 squadron moved in from Bottesford just after Christmas 1942, but the first Stirling to fly in crash landed as it slid into a ditch. Discretion appeared to be the better part of valour and the remainder of the squadron went back!

Eventually No 90 got down to business as a mine laying mission was performed on 8th January, 1943 the first of 52 missions from Ridgewell. Their targets ranged from French coast attacks to the engineering works in Turin, Italy the following month. The German capital of Berlin was bombed on 1 March 1943, as part of the bomber offensive played by No 3 Group.

The low altitude performance used by the Stirlings saw great courage necessary by the crewman, none more than Sgt Bill Davine who was terribly injured in the legs while at his post, but he refused to give in and continued to issue instructions for a second bomb run, and not until this was completed would he allow the aircraft to head for home despite severe damage.

At the end of May the RAF moved out and the 381st Bomb Group of the Eighth Air Force arrived, their B17 Flying Fortresses remaining at Ridgewell until the end of the war the only heavy bomber base in Essex.

After their first raid on Antwerp, tragedy hit the base the next day when a huge explosion killed 23 personnel and a civilian as the aircraft were being loaded for a mission.

The name of Schweinfurt will never be forgotten for on 17 August, 1943, no less than 11 aircraft failed to return, over 100 men, the largest loss on one mission by an Eighth Air Force group.

Targets all over Europe received calls from the Ridgewell group and on 25 April, 1945 No. 297 mission completed their tally. Even then death had the final word, when a B17 carrying over 30 men for a holiday in North Ireland crashed into a mountain on the Isle of Man killing all aboard this with less than a week of the war in Europe left.

Ridgewell was transferred back to the RAF when No. 94 MU stayed from September 1946 to March 1957.

Wethersfield

Wethersfield airfield opened as a RAF base in January 1944 but the USAAF were first to arrive when A20 Havocs of the 416th Bomb Group of the Ninth Air Force moved in.

They began similar operations to those carried out by the Gosfield group attacking railyards, and V-Bomb sites on the French coast, but as the war progressed the 416th also moved to forward bases, to Melun Villaroche near Paris.

After the Americans moved out the RAF took their places, with the Stirlings who had been badly mauled after Arnhem, Mark IVs of Nos 196 and 299 squadrons settled in training for gliding operations, but bad drainage problems at the base led to the squadrons moving out to Shepherds Grove in Suffolk.

Operation Varsity saw Wethersfield play its part when the Ninth Air Force C47 Dakotas lifted the 6th Airborne Division for battle.

In October 1945, the 1167 Target Towing Flight which had been at Gosfield moved in but disbanded in January 1946. During this time an ORTU equipped with Halifaxes and Stirlings arrived and became the 1385 Heavy Conversion Unit, but once they left in April 1946 the base became a Care & Maintenance Unit.

APPENDIX IV

ROLL OF HONOUR

'There is a victory in dying well for
freedom and you have not died in
vain'

Some parishes record only those
residents who fell while others recorded all those who served, +
indicating the fallen.

Halstead RIP

F. Allen — Essex Reg
G.W. Ardley — RN
F.W. Ashfield — RAF
Vic Banbury — RHA
P. Bartholomew — QRR
Eric Barwood —
Charlie Beckwith — RA
Duncan Brooks — RAF
F. Bush — RAF
Percy Constable — Essex Reg
Neville Chumbley — RA
Cedric Diss — RN
Tom Finch — RAF
Derek Gordon — RA
R.S. Gowers — Middx Reg
Leslie Granfield — Gren G.
J.W. Hall — RAF
M.W. Harrington — Beds & Herts
Hedley Iron — Glid Pil Reg
J.W. Jarman — Suff Reg
Maurice Kemp — Essex Reg
Mark Kibble — RA
Francis Knowles — RAF
Arthur Maskell — REME
Harold Meadows — Suffolk Reg
Peter Mitson — RAF
Walter May —
Leonard Nunn —
Tom Pilgrim — RA
Ron Rayner — Black Watch
Cyril Rowland — RAF
Robert Sargent — RAF
Fred Smith — RAC
R.W. Symonds — ACC
Frank Tempan — RAF
Ken Turp — RAF
Arthur Vitler — ROS
Douglas Whitfield — MN
E.J. Wicker — RAF

Alphamstone

Ashen

A. Beaumont
+ E.J. Bowers +
Jean Bowers
A. Brown
E.H. Bunting
W.R. Bunting
F. Eady
T.A. Eady
C.J. Eady
G.J. Eady
F.C. Eady
P.S. Elliott
G.C. Gibbons
C.H. Green
G.A.J. Greig
G. Hayes
R.F. Hayes
F.A. Hobby
R. Hobby
E.C. Howard
R.J. Jennings
A.W. Letch
W.J. Martin
C.R. Mortimer
J.T. Orbell
G.W. Orbell
S.G. Parker
A.J. Peacock
+ P.H. Peacock +
F. Elizabeth Praill
W. Stead
H.A.W. Swallow
Minna D. Thrower
Dorothy V. Turner
W.J. Wade
C.J. Wood
N.W. Wood

74

Belchamp St Paul
+ John Chatters +
+ Frederick Underwood +

Belchamp Otten
+ Fred Howard +

Belchamp Walter
+ J. Partridge +
+ A.H. Reeve +

Birdbrook

+ George Wilfrid Backler +
+ Frank Sidney Walter Cook +
+ Eric George Kendall +

Borley

Bulmer

+ Harry St. G. Burke +
+ Anthony Hyde Parker +
+ George B. Hawksley +
+ Herbert Raymond +

Bures

+ E.R. Boreham +
+ A.C. Brown +
+ K.P. Carr +
+ S.E. Clampin +
+ G.P. Garrod +
+ S.A. Gee +
+ H.J. Graves +
+ B.G. Mott +
+ A.C. Twitchett +
+ H. Warden +

Bomb victims

+ F.M. Eldred +
+ A.E. Willingham +
+A.G. Willingham+
+E. Willingham+

Castle Hedingham

+ Roy Ambrose +
+ Dennis Dowsett +
+ Eric Ravilious +
+ David Ruffel +

Colne Engaine

Gordon Atkinson
Cyril Ball
Bill Cook
Major George Courtauld
Cyril Cheeseman
Bill Deeks
David Griffiths
Paul Maytham
Gus Monk
Fred Partridge
Philip Pudney
Dick Rablin
+ Edward C. Schofield +
+ John L. Watson +
Gerald Watson
Peter Watson

Earls Colne

+ F. Cadman +
+ B. E. Harvey +
+ A. J. Higgleton +
+ L. C. James +
+ G. D. Nott +
+ R. Pakenham +
+ D. V. Willingham +

Foxearth

+Wilfred Farrance+

Gestingthorpe

+ D. W. Meeking +
+ John S. Philp +

Gosfield

+ Leonard Arthur Ketley +
+ David Howard Lowe +
+ Kenneth Sewell +
+ John Peter Turner +
+ Alfred Edward Williams +

Greenstead Green

+ John Cedric Addy — RAF +
+ Sydney Brookes — RAF +
+John Percival Butler — RAF+
+ Kenneth Edward Cook — RAF +
+ Harold Kitchener Larter —
   Essex Reg. +

Great and Little Henny

+ Alfred Charles Tuffin +

Helions Bumpstead

+ John Knox +

Lamarsh

Liston

Great and Little Maplestead

+ Cpl Arthur Parish — April 1942 +

Middleton

Bernard George Bryant
Frederick Bryant
+George William De Cort (R.I.P.)+
Alfred George Everett
George William Nice
Alfred Guy Weavers
Walter John Weavers
Madeleine Vera Weavers
Charles White
Eric White

Ovington

Pebmarsh

Pentlow

+ P.I.A. Plumb +
+ D.F. Smith +
+ George F. Chambers
   (Home Guard) +

Ridgewell

+ Francis Beane +
+ Ronald Bowden +
+ Lindsay Cann +
+ Patrick Mascall +
+ Ronald Wiffen +

Sible Hedingham

B.W.J. Abraham
D. Alliston
B. Ambrose
V.S. Ambrose
W.J. Andrews
E.R.W. Ashby
T. Ashby
W.H. Bacon
D.F. Baggaley
J.W. Baggaley
C.A. Barber
R. Barber
C.W. Bareham
E.W. Bareham
R.W. Bareham
D. Barker
P. B. Barker
D.A. Barningham
A. Bartlett
D.A. Beadle
E.E. Beadle
W.W. Beadle
J.E. Beaumont

A. Bell
E.C. Bell
J.F. Bell
L.G. Bell
C.M. Bickers
R.A. Bonner
B.E. Boreham
C.C. Boreham
D.F.G. Boreham
F.S. Boreham
H.C. Boreham
H.G. Boreham
J. Boreham
M.J. Boreham
S.G. Boreham
J.G. Borrett
L. Bowtell
G.R.F. Bradford
A.F. Brett
J.H. Brett
+ L.V. Brett +
A. Britton
M.S. Bruty
+ S.R. Bult +
C.W.G. Bullock
J.W. Butcher
L.W. Cansell
+ A.C. Carter +
A.D. Carter
Dorothy L. Carter
F.G. Carter
Nellie M. Carter
R.H. Carter
J. Cartwright
L.N. Catterwell
D. Chapman
K.G. Chatten
Dulcie J. Clark
G.D. Clark
W.G.S. Clarke
B. Clarke
A.B.D. Cock
Blanche D. Cock
Iris E. Cock
N.S. Cock
P. Cock

V.S. Connell
D.D. Copsey
Beatrice M. Corder
E. Corder
+H.J.W. Cousins+
J.G.D. Cowlin
R.A.F. Craven
B.W. Cutts
H. Dace
G.W. Daines
R. Daines
A.J. Deal
A.E. Dixey
D. Dowling
J. Dowling
P.H. Dowsett
D.C. Drury
R.H. Drury
S.R. Dyson
D.R. Earey
H.C. Earey
H.E. Earey
W. Eldridge
W.J. Ennew
C.R. Everitt
+ F.E. Everitt +
H.J. Everitt
H.J. Everitt
J. Everitt
P.W. Everitt
R.R. Everitt
V.A.W. Everitt
G.F. Faiers
J.H.E. Farrant
D. Faux
+ T.A. Firman +
D.A.E. Foster
S.R. Gardner
E.G. Geater
Isabel B. Gibson
Peggy E.M. Gibson
F.J. Gilbey
J.P. Gladwell
A.L. Gorringe
R.E. Greenway
+ C. Hale +

Phyllis M. Hale
S.R. Hale
A.F. Halls
C.A. Halls
M.B. Halls
W.P. Halls
D.R. Happe
C.R. Harper
R.E.J. Harper
W.C. Harrington
D.C.R. Harrod
S.L. Heard
Barbara J. Hockham
F. Hockham
C.G. Holden
A.W. Howard
C.M.H. Howe
Phyllis J.N. Hume
+ H.J. Iron +
H.R. Irvine
S. Jarvis
T. Jarvis
B.H. Kendall
G.L. Kendall
R.C. Kendall
A.F. Laver
K.E. Laver
S. Letch
S.W. Letch
R.G. Mailer
R.A. Mansfield
H.E. Martin
E. Mayhew
E.F. Mathews
Elsie K. Mead
C. Mead
S.G.A. Mead
S. Metson
F. Moles
J. Moles
Kathleen F. Moles
I. Murray
E.G. Needham
D.G. Newman
D.M. Newman
J. Nicholls

R. Nicholls
Joan B. Noble
J.H. Noble
D.E.J. Owens
A.H. Pannell
W.G. Pannell
S.G. Parsley
H. Pilgrim
R.D. Pilgrim
S.D. Pilgrim
R.A. Plaistow
S.A. Plumb
Iris M. Proudfoot
R.E. Pryke
+ W.A.J. Pryke +
F. Rayner
H.T.H. Rayner
P. Rayner
T. Redgewell
F.S. Repnan
H.J.H. Ripper
N.C. Ripper
C.H. Rippingale
C.B. Richer
O. Roberts
Lillian D. Robinson
H.E. Rose
+ R.E. Rose +
S.G. Rose
A.R. Ruffle
E. Ruffle
G.F. Ruffle
Gladys E. Ruffle
G. Kate Ruffle
J.W. Ruffle
S. Ruffle
S.F. Ruffle
W.A. Ruffle
B. Sandford
J.V. Scott
A.R. Skipp
W.R. Slee
J.B. Sloan
F.W. Smith
H.S. Smith
J.H. Smith

K.B. Smith
Nora Smith
P. Smith
P.D. Smith
R. Smith
R.G. Smith
W.F. Smith
H.L. Springett
J.W. Springett
R. Staines
A.R. Stockdale
S.R.R. Strudwick
J.J. Sutton
G.R. Tanner
F.J. Taylor
H. Taylor
J.L. Turner
V.J. Turner
Betty Vale
E.A. Vale
C.V. Wade
S.D. Walters
+ M.H. Ward +
G.A. Warner
B. Wells
F. Wells
T.R. Wells
W.A. Wells
B. Wheeler
R.D. Wheeler
K.W. Wilding
R.F. Wilding
W.E. Wilding
C.E.V. Williams
R. Williams
F.E. Willis
J. Winter
A.H. Wiseman
C. Wiseman
H.W. Wiseman
M.W. Wiseman
P.R. Wiseman
Eileen M. Woodcock
A.W. Worsfold
H.E. Worsfold
O.A.C. Wright

D.E. Yarham
P.R. Young

Stambourne

George Boughtwood
Ivor Debenham
Reuben Debenham
Arthur Ernest Drew
Douglas Halls
James Irish
Charles Metson
Frederick Mickley
Harry Mickley
'Chick' Rayner
William Roberts
Ronald Tarbin
George Towns
John Wesley

Steeple Bumpstead

+ Basil Boggis +
+ Stanley Clayden +
+ William Clayden +
+ Edward Harrison +
+ Malcolm Humphrey +
+ Leslie Ling +
+ Frederick Ling +
+ Harry Mizon +
+ Alec Pink +
+ Bruce Robson +
+ Leslie Tarling +
+ Reginald Wesley +
+ Harold Wesley +
+ Keith Haylock (CYPRUS) +

Sturmer

Tilbury-juxta-Clare

+ Royston V. Cox — Royal Signals +
+ Cecil E. Kemp — Herts Reg +

Toppesfield

Robert Allen
Jack Babbage
Ronald Chambers
Rosalie Chambers
Harry Chamberlain
Cyril Clark
+ James Clark +
Frank Clarke
Cyril Claton
Sidney Elsdon
Victor Everitt
C.A. Fitch
+ James Goodchild +
David Gould
Hubert Hardy
Sidney Hardy
Basil Hardy
Albert Letch
George Machen
E. Miller
Clifford Palmer
Jack Palmer
Maurice Pannell
Ernest Pannell
Victor Parmenter
Lewis Rollingson
Richard Ruggles
Cecil Smith
Jack Smith
Lionel Smith
Ronald Smith
+ Dennis Tarbin +
Jim Tarbin
Albert Tarbin
Winifred Tarbin
Herbert Unwin
Leslie Wash

Twinstead

White Colne

+ R. Bartholomew +
+ R. Leach +
+ R. Raymond +
+ J. Smith +

Wickham St. Paul

+ George Dyer Nott (33), RAC +

Great Yeldham

+ J. Alliston +
R. Alliston
C.D. Angel
J. Argent
F. Boreham
Beatrice L. Boyling
G. Brown
M. Brown
J. Bunton
A. Carter
J.W. Carter
D.G. Christison
D.S. Christison
F.A. Cobbold
F.M. Cole
H.L. Cooper
G.M. Cooper
J. Cossey
A. Courtauld
C.N. Daniels
F. Daniels
A.V. Deal
G.E. Dennis
F. Dowsett
C.K. Ellis
F. Fitch
Elsie Fulcher
F. Gallifant
+ L. Gibson +
+ W. Gibson +

+ G.J. Goodchild +
Grace Graham
A.F. Hall
J.R. Hasler
J.B.A. Hayter
C.G. Henderson
S. Jobson
H. Kemp
+ G.W. Louth +
J.M. Louth
H. Lowery
Jenny Lowery
S. Lowery
W. Lowery
A. Martin
D. Martin
J. Mayes
J.A. Moore
C.E. Nankivell
+ H. Osborne +
Catherine Quinan
E. Quinan
S. Quinan
J. Revell
R.W. Revell
R.C. Rice
S.W. Rice
+ J. Rogan +
J.G. Rogan
Mary Rose
J.B. Ruggles
M. Rulten
R.F. Rulten
H.J. Rulten
L. Rulten
A. Seymour
Phyllis Seymour
A. Smee
J.P. Snelling
+ G. Stebbing +
W.N. Stebbing
W. Steward
+ R. Stoker +
M. Sutton
+ C. Tarbin +

E. Tarbin
J. Tarbin
F. Turner
W. Turner
G. White

Little Yeldham

+ Ronald Smith — RAF +

Salute the Soldier

LITTLE YELDHAM!

PROGRAMME:

Saturday, May 13th.—American Baseball Match and Side-shows at Bendysh, 2.30 p.m. Running commentary of match on field by loud speakers.—Dance in Community Hall at 8 p.m. Admission 2s. Stanleys Band. Refreshments.

Monday, May 15th.—Comedy Concert. Lots of laughs with local talent at the School, 7.30 p.m. Guest Artist, " Comic Cutts."

Tuesday, May 16th.—Whist Drive at School, 7.30 p.m. Admission 1s. 6d. (including refreshments).

Friday, May 19th.—Dance. Community Hall, 8 p.m.; 2s. Stanleys Band. Refreshments.

Saturday, May 20th.—Grand Final Dance in Community Hall, 8 p.m. Admission 2s. American Band. Refreshments.

Sunday, May 21st.—Empire Youth Sunday. United Youth Service in the Church. 3 p.m. Address by R. Rulten (chairman of Youth Club). Youth Club Choir.

For further details see Posters.

Proceeds to be invested in War Savings for Village Hall Fund.

APPENDIX V

B Company 2/5th Battn, Essex Regiment — Territorial Army*

Battn Commander — Col Cedric Portway.
Company Commander — Capt Anthony Baldwin
(at 3rd September, 1939).

Bert Ambrose
Fred Arnold
Don Abbott
Bernard Andrews
Ron Bartholomew
Aubrey Barnes
Bert Bragg
Hazel Bragg
Bob Bragg
Sid Basford
Ted Beard
Aubrey Brown
Bill Brown
Ernie Brown
Fred Brown
Alf Binks M.M.
Ron Booty
John Beaney
Ken Bird
Sid Bullard
Roy Burfield
Wilf Clark
George (Soss) Cook
Eddie Cook
Philip Cook
Syd Coe
Bob Coe
Fred (Pimpy) Coe
Albie Coe
Harold Coe
Alf Cousins
Percy Constable
Don Cutmore
Jim Carter

Harold Daw
Jackie Diss
Sid Denny
Dennis Dowsett
Harold Earey
John Eldred
George Etherington
O'Villiers Fenner
Bob Fleuty
George Green
Bob Green
Roy Giller
Tom Gallifant
Eddie Heavingham
George Hostler
Bill Higgleton
Jerry Higgleton
Bill Howe (CQMS)
Jack Harrington
Eric Harrington
Eric Hardy
Rex Hardy
Peter King
Paul King
Ted King
Jackie Kensall
Dennis Lee
Paul Maytham (2nd Lt)
Bert Mildenhall
Ted Mortimer
Roy Outing
Fred Patmore
Dick Pakenham
Jim Porter (2nd Lt)

82

Jimmy Paulyn	Charlie Self
Fred Rose	Jack Stedman
Jimmy Ruggles	Len Tokeley
? Richardson	Maurie Wiseman
Charlie Rulton	Edgar Wiseman
Ken Root	D.J.B. Willingham
Dennis Root	Maurie Willingham
Fred (Nipper) Smith	Tom Wells
Albie Smith	Ron Wicker (CSM)
Rex Scillitoe	
Hubert Saunders	
Russell Saunders	*These men are some of those who
	served in B Company.

Halstead Urban District Council.

HOME-COMING of the FORCES

A PUBLIC MEETING

will be held at the

CO-OPERATIVE HALL, HALSTEAD,

on

WEDNESDAY, 23rd MAY, 1945, at 7 p.m.

Chairman: J. R. ROOT, Esq., J.P.

The Meeting has been called by the Council so that the Townspeople may consider the making of fitting arrangements for the Welcome Home of men and women of the Forces, and of raising monies to commemorate their service in the war.

Dated 12th May, 1945.   RONALD LONG,
                                                    Clerk to the Council.

APPENDIX VI

ABBREVIATIONS used in this book

A.R.P.,	Air Raid Precautions
A.T.C.,	Air Training Corps
Battn.,	Battalion
B.G.,	Bomb Group
C.M.P.,	Company Military Police
C.O.,	Commanding Officer
H.Q.,	Headquarters
H.Ex.,	High Explosive
H.R.D.C.,	Halstead Rural District Council
H.U.D.C.,	Halstead Urban District Council
K.I.A.,	Killed in action
M.I.A.,	Missing in action
N.A.A.F.I.,	Navy Army Air Force Institution
N.C.O.'s	Non Commissioned Officers
O.R.T.U.,	Officer Refresher Training Unit
P.O.W.,	Prisoner of War
R.D.C.,	Rural District Council
Regt.,	Regiment
R.A.F.,	Royal Air Force
S.O.E.,	Special Operations Executive
T.A.,	Territorial Army
U.D.C.,	Urban District Council
U.S.,	United States
U.S.A.A.F.,	United States Army Air Force
U.X.B.,	Unexploded Bomb
W.I.A.,	Wounded in action
W.V.S.,	Womens Voluntary Service

APPENDIX VII

WOMEN'S LAND ARMY

Women have always worked on the land the world over, but the idea of a 'Land Army' sprung up in the first World War, to produce food for the war effort while men were away.

During the summer of 1939, around half a million men worked the land, as did about 55,000 women, along with about 100,000 casuals of both sexes.

All types of girls, aged from about 18, many from industrial cities, made up the majority of the organisation, some getting homesick when working 'out in the sticks'.

By the end of November about 2,800 girls had been placed on the land since the outbreak of war. They underwent periods of training, mostly on the farms, but some at agricultural institutes, such as Chelmsford and Writtle in Essex, and Chadacre, near Bury St. Edmunds, in Suffolk.

During the period of training reports were often favourably received, and the farmer's experiment of employing the girls proved worthwhile.

The minimum wage for an 18 year old was 28/- a week (£1.40) for a 48 hour week, and for those under 18 it was 22/6, with overtime at 7d and 6d respectively.

Out of their wages the girls had to pay for their own board and lodging, as at Bois Hall, then later at Blue Bridge, Halstead. However where this was provided by the farmer, he deducted 14/- for board and lodging.

There was discipline, with girls expected home by 10pm, while a dismissal could mean a transfer to a munitions factory, obviously a target for enemy aircraft, something the girls did not relish.

The WLA uniform consisted of green jersey, brown breeches (often cut down to shorts), slouch hat, khaki overcoat and wellington boots for winter time.

Many were involved in horticultural work, glasshouses, taught to drive tractors, hoeing fruit and vegetables, fruit picking and planting, while some even turned their hand to rat catching!

There was even a Timber Brigade, responsible for providing pit props and telegraph poles. A dairy maid had to be up at 4 am, complete with torch and apron, groping round a pitch dark farmyard, subjected to ARP blackout regulations, only to fall over the stools and pails in the cowshed!

Just imagine a young girl attempting these tasks for the very first time, but needs must, and they just got on with it, and in the ned could match the men in almost every task.

The girls had little money to spend during their off duty hours, but one of the more pleasurable pursuits was invitations to dances, frequently by the Americans stationed at Gosfield airfield.

Some girls stayed in the area only a few months, but learned a multitude of tasks in the quiet fields of the Colne Valley, increasing their interest in country life.

Many of them married local men and stayed in the district, maintaining a lifelong friendship with the farmer and his family and recall the times that threw them together.

Quotes:-

Mrs Beat Smith (nee Williams) and mother of Halstead's mayor, Mrs Jackie Pell, remembers "Along with my sister Rose, we were billeted at Bois Hall, which stood off Sudbury Road, and taken round to the farms for the listed task of the day. Often we worked on farms at Pebmarsh or Colne Engaine, and I remember Ben Goodwin who was landlord of the Five Bells, and his wife, being very kind to us girls. There were hard times, with little washing facilities if we were working in the fields all day but we had some fun too and I like to think we learned a lot of useful things for later life".

Three other girls who also stayed on in Halstead, now Mrs Doreen Curtis, Mrs Joan Bugbee and Mrs Frances Alston, were all billeted at Blue Bridge. The building which still stands on the bank above the old garage, was originally to house Italian Prisoners of War and was one of the first building jobs the husband to be of Mrs Alston, John Alston, was engaged on when he started work for the late Jimmy Norton back in 1941.

Now living at Clacton, Mrs Evelyn Dixon, recalls her working days in the Kent fruit fields, saying "I can remember how we used to watch the dog fights in the sky during the Battle of Britain. Then there was the day I was picking apples up a tree when the tree split in half, damaged from an earlier air raid. The ladder went one way and I went the other, and ended up in Canterbury Hospital for a few weeks with a broken pelvis!"

The Women's Land Army line up at Blue Bridge, Back row left to right: Kathy Vincum, Marjorie Watson, Vera ?, Shelia ?, Mrs ? ?, (a cook), ? ?, Lilly Rodell, Celia ?, ? ?, ? ?, and Doreen Curtis. Centre: Irene Horne, Thelma Rivett, Violet ?, Edna McGregor, ? ?, Miss Mac ? (supervisor), ? ?, Frances Alston, Alice Waters and Hilda ?. Front: ? ?, Joe Stollery, Doris ?, Kathy Dodge, Maisie ?, ? ?, Doris ?, Joan Bugbee and Irene Wilson.

Rose Williams (left) and friend whilst serving in the Land Army at Bois Hall Farm, Halstead. In the background is Bois Hall Farm House which has long since been demolished. The Hall and adjacent farm buildings stood where Bois Hall Gardens Housing estate is now situated.